# FIGHTING
## TO THE DEATH

# FIGHTING
# TO THE DEATH

## MY LIFE IN THE WORLD'S DEADLIEST FIGHT GAME

### CARL MERRITT
#### with WENSLEY CLARKSON

JOHN BLAKE

Published by John Blake Publishing Ltd,
3 Bramber Court, 2 Bramber Road,
London W14 9PB, England

www.johnblakepublishing.co.uk

First published in paperback in 2009

ISBN: 978-1-84454-690-9

British Library Cataloguing-in-Publication Data:

A catalogue record for this book is available from the British Library.

Design by www.envydesign.co.uk

Printed in the UK by CPI Bookmarque, Croydon, CR0 4TD

3 5 7 9 10 8 6 4 2

Papers used by John Blake Publishing are natural, recyclable products
made from wood grown in sustainable forests. The manufacturing processes
conform to the environmental regulations of the country of origin.

Photographs courtesy of James Bareham (pp 4 and 8) and Graham Attwood (p5)

'He's got a time bomb waiting to go off in him, that one.'

*Nil By Mouth*, written and directed
by Gary Oldman, 1997

To Carole and my mum – where would I be without them?

# Contents

# Introduction

I first met Carl Merritt when Hollywood film director John Irvin suggested I speak to Carl about his experiences in the fight game. Irvin had used Carl as a consultant on his boxing flick, Shiner, starring Michael Caine. I knew little about Carl except that the sort of fights he got into sometimes ended in death. So it was with a certain amount of trepidation that I arranged to meet him in a West London pub.

It wasn't as if Carl was huge. He was about two inches shorter than my six foot one, but he was compact and incredibly solid looking in a Mike Tyson sort of way. Carl seemed embarrassed by what he'd done. There was none of that macho pride and boasting that I'd expected. He was a quiet, shy man who gave the impression of being a decent human being – not a bloodthirsty scrapper whose strength and determination had seen off many of the world's hardest characters. He clearly respected his fellow man, despite the brutal nature of his profession.

I watched Carl as he sized me up in much the same way he would size up an opponent in the moments before a fight. Then he winked at me and I knew we'd end up lifelong pals. For beneath the surface lies a thoughtful individual who knows people inside out and lives by more than just his brute strength. He told me, 'I study a person the first time I meet 'em. It doesn't take long – maybe a few minutes – and I soon suss out who's on my wavelength.' Luckily I passed that test.

But others were not so lucky; I glimpsed another side of Carl seconds after that first interview ended. A young yuppie-type bumped into him at the exit to the pub where we'd enjoyed a few pints. Carl stopped and turned, and in that one beat I saw an expression on his face that must have struck fear and trepidation into his opponents. It was a look that could have ended in his breaking a dozen bones in that other man's body in a matter of seconds.

Carl stared at the yuppie as he passed by and then looked at me for encouragement. The hairs on the back of my neck stood on end: I ignored his response without comment, aware that if I'd acknowledged what had happened then the tap marked 'red mist' would have been turned full on. Instead, I held the door open, encouraged Carl to leave the pub and breathed a quiet sigh of relief.

The violence within Carl is always simmering close to the surface. You can see it in the way he reacts if he spots anyone looking in his direction. As a child all the trust was knocked out of him and from then on he looked on other males as a threat to his life and that of his beloved family. But these days he's somehow got that inner rage under control. Many may still call him a 'psycho' and a 'lunatic' but he's worked hard to beat those demons – or so we both hope.

Carl is not a showman like the late bare-knuckle king Lennie 'The Guv'nor' McLean. He's not a villain like the Krays or a nutter like 'Mad' Frankie Fraser. He's a master craftsman who knows the art of brutality inside out.

But you cross him at your peril ...

Wensley Clarkson
2009

# Foreword

My name's Carl Merritt. I'm sure you haven't heard of me, but by the time you've finished reading this book you won't ever forget who I am. I was born and bred in Forest Gate, East London. I survived in that tough environment by always keeping one step ahead, never letting anyone take the mickey.

I'm not a great one for going on about the past. 'The good old days', as some call them, don't really exist in my book. What's the point in rambling on about things when it's hard enough surviving today while keeping an eye on the future? I've always looked to my next move, not the last one or the one before that. All of the old boys I've come across keep their mouths shut about what they've been up to. That's the way it is where I come from.

But when I got together with Wensley and started talking about my life it dawned on me that all the things that have happened to me serve a purpose because they helped shape my life. A lot of the memories were painful to talk about after all these years, but as my mind started to buzz I began to realise that perhaps my story can serve as a lesson to any young tearaway who thinks he's had it hard and has no choice but to get into trouble. To them I say think again, there's always a way out of mischief, even if it means keeping on your toes so as to avoid the characters who want to own you and hold onto you.

Down the years I've been asked to help out with people's problems on my manor. I've even given single mums money when they've been up against it because you gotta help people when they're down. You never know when it might be you who's up against all the elements.

That's not to say I haven't done a few bad things in my life but, hand on heart, I never hurt anyone who didn't deserve it. When I was a kid I knocked around with same right nutters who'd rob their own grannies as soon as look at them. But I didn't live by their code. I wanted to make it in the real world, not the underbelly of life where it's all such a desperate fucking scramble for survival.

In many ways I'm lucky to still be alive, even though I never broke a law that really mattered in my whole life. But however hard I tried to make a living on building sites, as a nightclub doorman and later in the fight game, the bad pennies kept coming back to haunt me. In the end they built me up as a tasty fighter inside the cage and I became the number one scrapper – the biggest hitter in the east. Trouble was those same characters owned me and used me.

The cage became in many ways a perfect mirror reflection of my life and there was only ever one way to get out of it – by hammering my opponent into the ground. That meant I did some things I now regret. But they had to be done. I had no choice. Otherwise I'd have ended up six feet under.

People like me are built to try and beat the system. I never crumble under pressure. But as a result I became, in a sense, two people. One was the big, strong tough guy who struck fear into opponents across the globe. The other me was a quieter, more thoughtful fella who desperately wanted to provide for his wife and children.

As I've said, I never knowingly hurt an innocent person but if anyone touches my family or friends I'll hunt them down and do the business. But don't get me wrong – I'm not a brooding eye for an eye, tooth for a tooth merchant. That's just a waste of energy. Revenge. It's a word that can burn away your soul and split your heart in two. No doubt about it. Revenge doesn't pay the bills. Revenge doesn't help you stay in love. Revenge doesn't create a happy family. Revenge just eats up everything in its wake.

I should know, as it's the driving force behind the story of *Fighting to the Death*. And because we all would like a measure of revenge at some time in our lives I think it's worth setting out my story.

Carl Merritt
2009

# Author's Notes

I've changed some names to protect (as they say) the innocent and not-so-innocent and myself. But the incidents are all true; there's been no need to invent anything. In fact, the difficulty has been to decide what to leave out!

C.M.

# Introduction

I t was a bitterly cold winter's day and the icy wind was burning into my cheeks as I struggled along the street towards my family home. I was fifteen years old and desperate to escape into the real world, earn a living and get on with my life.

As I ran up the path to our house, I heard screaming and shouting – a familiar sound that had so often filled my childhood. My mum was yelling about something or other with my 'stepdad' Terry. She was really giving him a hard time. Probably about his bad temper again or maybe he'd gone and disappeared for a few days as he sometimes did when he was up to no good.

I stopped at the entrance to our front door and took a deep breath. Did I really want to walk into yet another row after the sort of day I'd just had at school? I was tempted to turn round and head off for the open space of Wanstead Flats and my little hideaway amongst the trees and bushes where me and my mates would escape the pressures and unhappiness of our homes. But that day it was too bloody cold so I steeled myself for the usual verbal abuse and pulled out my door key.

My hand was shaking like a leaf. Was it the cold or the fear that I was about to walk into a war zone? After a couple of seconds I managed to steady my hand enough to slide the key into the Yale lock. Just then a male voice screamed: 'You fuckin' bitch. Don't you ever fuckin' talk to me like that!'

Then I heard the unmistakable thud of a fist connecting with flesh. That snivelling little piece of shit, Terry, was at it again.

Now my mum was crying and screaming at the same time. It was a horrible, disturbing blend of noises.

'You want more? You fuckin' want more?' he yelled.

'I hate you! I hate you! I hate you!' came my mum's reply.

I pushed open the door and ran towards the kitchen. Mum's face had blown up like a balloon and I immediately knew what he'd done to her. I stood there for a few moments not sure how to react. My mum turned away to try and stop me seeing the state of her face. Terry looked down at the floor in order to avoid my gaze.

My eyes narrowed to try and stop the tears of anger welling up. Without saying another word, I ran straight at Terry, whacked him in the face and then followed up with a flurry of right hooks. He cowered down to try and stop the punches connecting but he was no match for the sheer force of my anger.

The sound of my fists pounding into his body permeated the kitchen. It continued: tap ... tap ... with my left fist. As I pushed my arms away from my body, my bastard 'stepdad' took a swing at me and missed because I ducked too fast for him.

Then I popped a vicious right into his battered leathery face. It felt like a hard shot and he quivered after I connected. That's when I really steamed into him: left, left ... and then right ... WHACK; left, left ..., right ... WHACK; left, left ... right ... WHACK. Air wheezed out of him with every punch.

My mum looked on, aware that the shots I was targeting on her partner were going to stop him ever hurting her again. We both knew it was time to finish off this arsehole for good.

I finally stepped back as he crumpled to the floor. Then he looked up at me with an expression of sheer hatred on his face. He seemed to be about to get up and come at me again.

'Don't move,' I screamed at him.

But he ignored me and continued getting up from the floor. 'I said, "Don't fuckin' move!"'

But he wasn't listening and began veering in my direction. I grabbed a pen off the sideboard and faced him, with it clutched in my left hand.

He got even closer.

So I stuck the pen right in the side of his stomach and felt the squelch as it oozed through flesh and fat. I didn't mean to do it. It was just a defensive action. I pulled it out with all my strength and found myself staring down at the bloody pen in the palm of my hand. Moments later Terry doubled up in agony. I stood as he fell onto all fours on the floor and began crawling towards the door. I looked down at him for a few more seconds while he slithered into the hallway. Then I stepped forward and kicked him hard as he stumbled down the steps.

Good riddance!

I didn't care. He deserved it.

# CHAPTER ONE

# Sort of East-Enders

I was born in Forest Gate Hospital in east London on 22 September 1965. My mum Val and dad John lived in a tiny two-bed flat at the time. Mum's always saying I was a bloody huge baby when I popped out. I screamed and fought my way out of her and I've been doing the same thing in life ever since. Forest Gate is right on the edge of the old East End and that's the way I've always felt – right on the edge of things. Not many people know this area unless they've lived there. It's the sort of place you don't bother going to without a real reason. We don't get a lot of tourists up our way and they say the people east of Finsbury Park and north of Lambeth are different from anywhere else.

My mum told me once that Forest Gate was 'invented' when the railway rolled east from Liverpool Street to developments of houses for middle-class commuters more than a hundred years ago. At first the Quakers constructed the houses, so there were hardly any boozers as they were fiercely anti-drink. Back in those days cows still grazed in front gardens overlooking Wanstead Flats. About the most famous bloke to come from Forest Gate was the actor and film director Bryan Forbes and some fella who wrote the music for *The Sound of Music*. Just about sums this place up really.

After the last war lots of new buildings were constructed in the town centre. These days, Forest Gate is part of the borough of Newham and contains churches, mosques, Sikh and Hindu temples and a cross-section of inhabitants that cover just about every race and nationality in the world.

Traditionally, people move out of places like Forest Gate as soon as they make a few bob but my family never earned a decent enough wedge to make the great escape. If I tried to paint a picture now of what it was like I'd say there weren't many monuments to the past in Forest Gate. Its history seemed a kind of black void to me when I was a kid.

I recall row upon row of redbrick box houses plus tenement buildings from the Victorian days. There was the pleasant whiff of dough from a big bakery that employed many people. But the other, more constant smell came wafting across Forest Gate from the smelt works in nearby Wapping.

Once upon a time places like Forest Gate, Stepney, Bow, Bethnal Green and Mile End were posh commuter villages with fine houses and rich inhabitants. But those days were long gone by the time my mum and her family set foot in East London.

When I was born, my mum already had John, who was a year older. A couple of years after me, Ian arrived followed by Valerie (we all call her Lee) five years later. She was the baby of the family. We were all healthy, lively little rascals in our own different ways. My dad John was a plumber by trade, but he didn't always get enough of that kind of work. He'd do just about anything to earn a few bob. When I was a toddler, Mum and Dad seemed like everyone else's parents. I was too young to realise that all the racket I heard each night wasn't just coming from our black-and-white telly. Looking back on it, I hardly ever saw Mum and Dad happy together.

Mum was born in Silvertown in the heart of the old East End. Her mum died giving birth to her, so you can imagine how important we were to her. Her father had been a British military copper over in Italy at the end of the war when he married her mother – she was of Romany gypsy descent – and they had moved back to London, where Mum was born. My grandfather then joined the Met as a copper and my two uncles on Mum's side are still with the cozzers to this day.

My mum – all four feet eight inches of her – always had quite a mouth on her. Might be something to do with the fact that she had to scream to get any attention as a baby. When she beams, her Italian smile lights up the room, but when she's angry it brings more than thunderclouds on the horizon.

Dad was born in Canning Town, in the heart of the real East End. His mum was from Ireland and his dad was a German prisoner of war who had been locked up in Kent in a POW camp. Grandad was a cabinet-maker and still is one to this day. Dad's a big lad with huge shoulders, and has always kept very fit. He was much taller than I ever grew although now he's got a bit of a beer belly. Smokes roll-ups. But he's hung onto his own hair, unlike the rest of us, and seems to live in jeans, complete with long-sleeved shirts and Chelsea boots, most of the time.

Dad was always either out at work or up the local boozer, supping a few too many pints with his mates. Then he'd crash through the front door of our tiny flat, yelling at the top of his voice. That's when the fireworks usually started going off.

But then my parents had gone and married at such a young age. Mum was just sixteen when she had my brother John. My dad was in his early twenties. The pressure was enormous and they were just a couple of kids. It was never going to be easy.

Mum's family were all a bit upset when she went up the aisle with Dad. By then they had conveniently forgotten the shotgun that had been pointed in both Mum and Dad's direction when Mum told them she was pregnant. I reckon Dad's dodginess rubbed off a bit on my mum. He was from a huge family that consisted of more than twenty brothers and sisters. Mum seemed to deliberately go the other way from the rest of her law-abiding family. I think she got a few wallops for her troubles when she was a kid, so she ended up with little or no respect for the long arm of the law.

There were plenty of old characters on my manor when I was growing up. They were mainly Jack-the-lad types but they'd always help you out if you were in a spot and I learned a lot from them. They weren't necessarily villains but they were always there if you had any bother. Back then if you wanted a cup of sugar, or a lot more besides, you could always knock on someone's door. Everyone liked to stop and have a chat in the street. People's front doors were nearly always left open.

There was a corner shop near us called Clayton's that sold just about everything from ice lollies to baked beans. You could always get things on tick at old man Clayton's place. He had the tastiest sliced ham straight off the bone. It melted in your mouth. I was always in and out of the shop doing errands for my mum.

Old Mr Clayton was a real gent. He knew all the kids' names as well as the adults'. He'd first opened the shop during the last war and I suppose most of the business back then must have been through ration vouchers and stuff like that. By the time I was growing up on the manor, Mr Clayton was in his seventies but still as sharp as a tack. He was such a decent person he'd never tell a customer they owed money on tick in front of anyone else. Instead, he'd stop kids like me in the street ever so casually and say, 'Tell your mum I need to see her.' He was always giving me handfuls of sweets, especially if mum had just paid her bill.

When I went on my first day to St James's Infant School, aged five, I had to be dragged screaming from our house because I didn't want to leave home. My two brothers didn't seem to find it so tough, but I had a real problem getting along with other kids. I was a loner and I've stayed that way ever since. It's stupid when I think back on it now, but I just didn't want to go to school at all.

About the only thing I did learn in infant school was that it didn't matter what colour a person's skin was – if you liked 'em that was all that counted. I found myself sitting in a class with black, brown, yellow – you name it – and I judged them all the same. Pretty quick I got close to two black kids called Alex and Fraser. Later, I realised that the reason I got on so well with black people was that they knew what it was like to be the outsiders – and that's how I've felt all my life.

Compared to many of my mates back in those days, I was lucky really. At least there was a good atmosphere in the house when my mum was home. We all got on well and she taught me the importance of respecting other people – not to get in their face and cause aggro.

It has to be said we ware something of an accident-prone family. My baby sis, Lee, broke her arm in a playground, brother Ian got run over by a milk float but lived to tall the tale, and there were countless household scraps, but nothing any worse than what other families suffered.

I suppose the TV was my very best friend during much of my childhood. My favourite programme was *The Sweeney*. I loved losing myself in all that cops-and-robbers action. I'd be glued to the sat for hours on end. Naturally, round where I came from, it was the robbers who were our heroes. I also loved *Tom and Jerry*. I used to get really close to the telly and watch it on my own. Sometimes I'd talk back to some of the characters on the box. They seemed a lot nicer than many of the people I came across.

Then my mum went and ruined it all by making me and my brothers join the local cub pack. She thought it'd be good for us to get out and about. But being a bit of a loner, I didn't react well to any form of discipline. Worse still, a lot of the other kids were snotty towards us because we couldn't afford the full cub kit.

The only good time we ever had was when we want on a weekend camping trip to the Lake District. But then my brother John fell in the water from a canoe and I had to dive in and rescue him. I felt really proud to have saved him. But when we got back to London the cub master didn't even bother saying goodbye to us, which made me feel that none of them really cared.

The last straw came when an older cub took a nasty dislike to me and fired pot-shots at me with an air-rifle when I walked out of the scout hall one day. I got three pellets in my backside. I naturally made out I was close to death so that Mum would let me quit the cubs: it worked a treat. I was much happier back on my own.

From about the age of seven my best mate was a kid called Jason Neill, the son of a well-known local ducker and diver called Ron Neill. I suppose I was dead jealous of Jason because his dad was around most of the time and was always handing out tenners and fivers to us kids. That was a hell of a lot of money to a poverty-stricken nipper like me. Ron Neill seemed to have money spilling out of every pocket.

The Neills lived in a much bigger house than anyone else I knew. Jason and I got up to so much mischief together that they had to separate us in class. He was essentially a shy kind of kid like me, but with more money. Jason had a really expensive pushbike, which made me green with envy every time I saw it.

Nearby Wanstead Flats provided a perfect retreat – a brilliant haven for boys like me and Jason. We'd take our toy pistols with us and have imaginary fights. We pretended we were soldiers trained to the peak of our ability. We were often out until after dark on the Flats, which is something no parent would allow these days. Jason and I even took specially prepared 'survival kits', consisting of a bar of chocolate and a soggy cheese sandwich.

We loved laying small traps hidden under a covering of leaves so that anyone who walked over it would be caught by a piece of string and then mud would flick at them. Jason loved digging holes so deep that anyone walking along the pathway would lose their footing and crash to the ground. We used to hide in nearby trees and laugh our heads off watching them.

Eventually Jason and me made our own secret treehouse, in amongst the woods of the Flats. It was a three-pronged platform built between three massive oak trees. We'd sit in that treehouse for hours watching the traffic flow past a hundred yards away. We were both obsessed by cars back in those days. Jason's dad had a brand new, flashy Toyota. But Jason said what he really wanted was an Aston Martin, just like James Bond. I kept quiet about the fact my mum couldn't even afford a Ford Escort. As the cars drove past we had a competition to see who could name the make of car the fastest. We knew all the different models, even down to the engine sizes. 'I knew a 2000E Cortina from a 1600 just by the sound of the engine.

One day Jason and me spotted the handlebars of a motorbike in the main pond on the Flats. We pulled the bike out of the water to find it was virtually brand new. Obviously someone had nicked it and then dumped it. We spent hours trying to kick-start it and then gave up and pushed it back into the pond for good measure.

At the same time each Saturday, dozens of model airplane and boat operators would swarm onto the Flats. My mates and me used to rub mud on our faces and pretend we were on special patrol through the woods. Then we'd settle ourselves in the treehouse and have a right laugh watching the planes crashing into the woods nearby. We'd run over to where they'd crashed, and start winding up the owners as they knelt over their broken model planes, saying, 'That's a rubbish plane that one. You should go for something dearer next time.' They'd get really cheesed off.

One time me and Jason found an old air gun in a cupboard in his house and lugged it onto the Flats to take pot-shots at the model airplanes. The idea was to pretend they were Nazi bombers coming over to destroy our homes just like the real things had done in the East End thirty years earlier. It was only when Jason pulled the airgun out of a bag that we realised it might be a real shooter. It seemed heavy enough and it smelt of oil and grease. It turned out to have just two bullets in it and we shot them into a tree nearby. I nearly fell over when it came to my turn. We were bloody lucky no-one was hurt. I've never forgotten the terror I felt shooting that weapon. Then we sneaked it back into the cupboard at Jason's house just before the old man came back. Years later I realised he was probably holding on to that shooter for some blagger to use in a robbery.

The following weekend we stuck to more simple games such as laying obstacles on the runway used to land the model airplanes. That caused a right load of chaos and we nearly got our ears clipped when one owner spotted us running from the scene: but if we'd used that real shooter on the model aeroplanes, God knows what would have happened.

Jason and me used to hold pretend trial biking competitions on Wanstead Flats. All it really involved was jumping over ditches on our bikes but we both always ended up coming home covered in cuts and bruises. One day Jason and I were out playing on the Flats when he told me his mum and dad were always fighting. It's a bit twisted to admit it, but that made me feel better. So I wasn't the only one with fucked-up parents.

A few days later I called at Jason's and a stranger answered the front door and said that Jason and his mum had gone away and wouldn't be coming back. I was very upset. How could he just take off without saying a word? What sort of friend did that?

Not long afterwards, his dad Ron came barging his way into our house asking me if I knew where Jason and his mum had gone. I said I hadn't got a clue, which was true. 'You lying to me, son?' he asked sternly. I shook my head so furiously it almost came off its hinges. Then my mum chipped in, 'Of course he's telling the truth.' It was only then I realised they'd scarpered to get away from Ron. It turned out Ron had whacked his wife and then got so violent she'd decided to do a permanent runner.

Here we were living in a hovel with barely the money to pay the bills but at least we weren't on the run from a psycho dad. And you know what? Ron Neill never did find Jason or his mum and he ended up drinking himself to death just a few months later. They reckon he also died of a broken heart.

My mum often had music on in our flat. She loved all that sixties stuff like Ray Charles, The Temptations and most of the Motown artists of the day. Not surprisingly, I ended up being a big Stevie Wonder fan. Every weekend Mum had the record player on full blast all day, even during Sunday lunch. That's when my dad would retreat to the local boozer and stay there for most of the day while we tucked into sausages and roast potatoes.

In those days, Mum and Dad had a boozy party about once a month with their mates. It was the only time they seemed happy together. We were allowed to stay up late and often we'd nick a few peanuts, crisps and those miniature sausages on sticks, and sneak them into our bedroom. Our parents were the life and soul of those parties – thinking of those evenings brings back happy memories.

Then one day Dad announced he'd been offered some building work up north in Yorkshire and we'd all have to move up there pronto. The old man claimed it was much cheaper to live there. But within a couple of months he'd lost his job so we all trooped back down south with nowhere to live and ended up in a homeless hostel. Then my dad went and did a runner.

For about two weeks Mum, my brothers and me lived in that crummy hostel not knowing where our next square meal was coming from. I remember one night I was woken up by a strange scratching noise. Then something brushed my toes. It was a big, fat grey rat. I jumped out of my skin. I've never liked rodents since.

Mum and us three kids were huddled in that hostel all alone and very desperate. Then Dad came trooping back one day as if nothing had happened and announced he'd got us an upstairs council flat in Station Road, Forest Gate. It felt like Buckingham Palace after that hostel. But with two bedrooms it was a tight squeeze, to say the least.

But the old man's happy-go-lucky mood didn't last long. One night – I was about eight at the time – me and my brothers were tucked up in bed when Mum and Dad started one of their regular shouting matches. I lay there trembling as the yelling got louder and louder. John and Ian were fast asleep on the bottom bunk bed, but I couldn't get any shuteye because of the noise. Suddenly, I heard something break. It sounded like a vase or a bit of crockery. Anyhow, I leapt down to the floor from the top bunk and headed over to the door.

'Come here, you fuckin' bitch!'

My dad sounded completely out of control. I ran down the corridor and got to the top of the stairs. My tiny little mum came dashing out of the lounge. The old man was on her tail, towering over her.

They hadn't spotted me. That's when my dad lifted his arm as if he was about to whack my mum. He seemed like a giant to me back then. He was six feet one and fit as a fiddle, and Mum seemed so small up against him. I puffed up my chest and shouted at the top of my voice: 'Leave her alone!' The old man was so shocked his arm stopped in mid air. Tears were rolling down my mum's puffy, reddened cheeks.

I flew down the stairs and stood right between them. But then they started ranting and raving at each other again. My mum reached up over me and slapped my dad right across the face. He didn't respond but simply turned around and walked towards the bedroom. The flat went deathly quiet. A few moments later he emerged from the bedroom with a sports bag in his hand.

I followed my mum around the house as she shouted and screamed at him. In a way, I suppose I'd decided she needed protection. But, on reflection, she did go a bit over the top at him.

Then my older bruv John appeared and began begging my dad not to go, John and younger bruv Ian were in floods of tears and both hung onto Dad's trouser legs as he headed down the corridor towards the front door.

'I've gotta go, boys, I've had enough,' he told them while glancing back at my mum standing, hands on hips, watching him from the kitchen doorway. I stood back and observed the scene. Of course I was sad but I was more worried about my mum at the time.

The truth is my mum and dad had never really got on. These days they're reasonable friends. You've gotta remember Dad was still young, with lots of kids. The pressure must have been unbearable in many ways. A few days later he came round to tell us exactly what had happened and why he'd left, but it didn't make it any easier to handle.

At least Dad never laid another finger on Mum. She told me later that he was so shocked by my appearance that night, it made him stop and think about what had been going on between them. That's when he'd decided it was time to call it a day. But you know what? I'm not proud of what I did because sometimes I think that if I'd kept out of it, he'd still be my fulltime dad to this day.

Back then the old man was still struggling to get employment as a plumber, so he started working the doors at some right dodgy clubs in the East End. No doubt he was up to mischief, earning a bob or two from ducking and diving. And there's no denying he had a temper on him, but he was no worse than most dads round where I lived. The nastiest thing he ever did to me was when I got a bit lippy with him and he hauled me up by my ankles and started slapping my backside. It didn't half hurt. But then I'd deserved it for being a pain in the neck, like most kids.

It's a shame I don't have better memories of Dad. They are summed up by the time he came to visit me when I had my tonsils out in hospital. I must have been eight going on nine and the old man gave me an Action Man as a get-well present. Bloody thing was obviously second-hand because a few minutes after he'd left the hospital the head snapped off. I was so upset I cried myself to sleep that night.

But thankfully my dad never went for me or my brothers and

sister Lee, who was born just after my dad walked out. It was him and my mum who had the punch-ups. After they split, he'd come round once or twice a month and take us all out for a day trip to places like the Tower of London. He tried his hardest, but he never really said much and I can't honestly say he ever gave me one real word of advice the whole time I was a kid, which isn't saying much, is it?

Meanwhile, me and my mates in Forest Gate started getting up to our own brand of mischief. We'd pop over the wall of the local boozer, the Angel, nick a few empty beer and pop bottles and then bring them back into the pub's off-licence to claim the value of the empties. We used to get sixpence a go, which was very useful dough for an eight-year-old, I can tell you.

Then Mum and us kids got transferred by the council to a virtually new house just around the corner from our flat, even nearer to the vast green pastures of Wanstead Flats. It was really posh compared to what we were used to and my house-proud mum always kept it clean. But none of that stopped me and my brothers from causing havoc in the neighbourhood.

One day we almost got pinched by the local law after nicking some of Mum's stockings and putting them over our heads, grabbing a couple of toy guns and pretending to stick up the local newsagent. The owner, Mr Patel, blew his top when he realised it was a prank by a bunch of kids. We were only saved because Mum wandered in for a packet of Silk Cut just after we'd got caught. She gave us a right tongue-lashing following that little escapade.

After my dad went walkabout, a few 'new dads' appeared on the horizon so my brothers and sister (Lee was only a baby then) spent a lot of our time over on Wanstead Flats. Our

**14**

experience of Dad had not exactly made us very keen on any grown men entering the household. We saw them as a threat to our happiness.

Wanstead Flats was like an escape hatch for me and my brothers. We called it the countryside, even though it was only a couple of streets from home. It seemed like another world. Lots of green grass, a pond and huge, tall trees where we could shelter from the rain. It was paradise, really. I don't know how we'd have survived life at that time without the Flats.

Back at home, Mum held down at least two jobs to keep the family together, cleaning offices in the day and working behind the bars of local pubs in the evenings. Sometimes we had a baby-sitter but most of the time we fended for ourselves. Yet despite Mum's absences, we still lived in a loving home. I never felt abandoned, nor did my brothers or sister. We were gritty survivors. It was us against the world and we were going to win.

At one stage back then, we were so skint that we literally didn't even have a tin of beans in the kitchen cupboard. They were pretty desperate times. In those days Mum regularly visited the local loan shark who played a vital role in our survival. He even sometimes helped my mum carry her shopping back to our house because he lived nearby.

Everybody knew this fella so I won't embarrass him by naming him here. Mum had to pay him back loans on a weekly rate but often he didn't even charge her any interest. I remember one week she couldn't pay him a penny and he said not to worry and just added it up later.

The loan shark was a popular man on my manor. He was

always immaculately dressed in a Crombie coat and I was friendly with his kids. These days that sort of fella would probably be a drug dealer, which would have made him a completely different cup of tea.

Some weeks we were so broke we had candlelit dinners because Mum couldn't pay the electricity bill. And if we went and asked her for a few pennies for a few sweets and she said no. We knew not to ask her again that week. We certainly appreciated the value of money at an early age.

But even though she was often without a penny to her name, my dear old mum made sure our home was always immaculately tidy. And we always looked neat and pristine when we went out the front door. Us kids even nicknamed her 'Mrs Sheen' after the adverts on the telly because she always seemed to have a duster in her hand.

My main priority – even back then when I was only a youngster- was to earn a few bob. The pub where my mum worked sometimes paid me a couple of quid to stack the shelves with bottles before opening time. We were all expected to muck in and keep the family afloat.

Sometimes we nicked milk off the milk float plus a loaf of bread and some eggs if the kitchen cupboard was bare. We knew Mum was up against it and we tried to contribute even if it involved a bit of minor tea-leafing.

When I was about eight I got a police escort home after the cozzers nabbed me and a few mates when we threw stones from the roof of a nearby derelict building. My mum had watched the entire episode from her kitchen window and she was well upset when the PC dropped me home and explained what had happened. Mum didn't want me getting into the same habits as my dad. Poor old thing, she was trying her hardest to keep us all in order, but it wasn't easy with four kids and no support.

Me and my mates got up to all sorts. One of our favourite stunts was to tie some cotton thread round a milk bottle, put it on a wall and then spread the thread across the pavement so that whoever walked through it would end up sending the bottle smashing to the ground. We used to set up three or four milk bottles on one stretch of pavement round the corner from my home. It was bloody funny because people used to think that bottles were being thrown at them. But we always made sure we never did it to any old dears because they might not have been able to handle it.

In junior school, the first proper fight I got into happened when one boy called Delroy Walker tried to give me a hammering. He seemed like a giant compared to me. (He's now a preacher near where I live and he's always trying to get me to turn up at church on a Sunday. Not on your life, mate!) But as he goaded me, something came over me. I became completely fearless, steamed in and jabbed him hard in the neck and face, and down he went like a sack of spuds. The fight was over virtually before it had begun. I'd never felt such anger before in my life. I suppose it was an outlet for all the problems that had been building up for so long.

I was hauled in front of the headmaster, Mr Atkins, and given two whacks with a ruler, right across the palm of my right hand. It bloody hurt and left two big lines. When I got home, my mum went mad. She didn't like anyone laying a finger on any of her boys. She grabbed me by the ear and marched me across the road to the school and demanded that the headmaster explain why he'd punished me. He seemed terrified of her and even said he was sorry.

My mum still reckons to this day that I don't know my own strength. She's never forgotten how I split my kid brother's forehead when I chucked a plastic cup at him from twenty feet away. But that school fight helped persuade Mum to let me join the local boxing club, West Ham Boys' Club, in Plaistow. She wasn't keen on her kid being given a battering, but it was better than letting me wander the streets causing aggro. She knew I needed some kind of outlet for all my pent-up anger and frustration.

CHAPTER TWO

# Earning Respect

I loved it down at West Ham Boys' Club because it was like an escape from all the problems at home and school. Boxing gave me a lot of pleasure and a real sense of achievement. I was fitter than most of the other kids because I was regularly running three miles, from home to the club, to save money on the bus fare.

Boxing became my main interest in life. School was a waste of time and I didn't take to most other sports – especially team games. I was so fixated on boxing, I'd stay behind late at the gym and watch other, older fighters and study their form. I even had a notebook in which I drew pictures of the ways they stood and the ways they punched. I wanted to be better than any of them and I was prepared to train myself. I really believed boxing could lift me out of the slums.

At home, I was still constantly glued to the telly, but now

watched the boxing on the BBC. Whenever they showed any of the old Ali fights I'd go into a trance and study every movement. My mum, brothers and sister would come home and I wouldn't even notice them. I started trying to copy Ali's technique and I'd stand up and shadowbox while watching him on the TV out of the corner of my eye. Down at West Ham Boys' Club, they weren't keen on a kid doing the Ali-shuffle routine because it meant I didn't keep my guard up all the time, which was against all the training rules for a young fighter. So I did it when none of the coaches were watching.

There were times when I went completely over the top during matches at the club. I'd get all pent up with tension during sparring and sometimes ended up being dragged off my opponent still punching away well after the bell had gone. That sort of behaviour got me a bit of a reputation at the club as well as with a lot of the other kids on the manor. The nasty ones were always trying to wind me up so I'd lose it and punch out their biggest enemies. Not surprisingly. I didn't always keep my cool.

One time I walked out of the club in a bit of a bad mood because I'd lost to a sparring partner, which didn't happen often, and the kid who'd beaten me was standing there with a few of his pals as I walked past. He called out at me, 'When you joinin' the Girl Guides then?' I tried to ignore him at first because I knew it was a wind-up. Then he had another dig, 'Poor little Carl. No bottle, eh?' That was it. No one accused me of being a coward and got away with it.

I was standing a few yards from him so I aimed my gym bag right at his face. That distracted him for long enough to give me a chance to get nearer. I was soon climbing over two of his mates to get at him. I put a sharp left down on his forehead, while those two other kids tried to hold me back. Bull's-eye.

My opponent reeled back and tried to slap out at me wildly but couldn't get near enough. I caught him with another powerful left that sent him reeling backwards. Just then a couple of the dads and trainers walked out. One of them immediately realised what had happened and lost his rag. He gave us both a good slap round the face. We deserved it. And then he cracked our heads together for good measure. 'Behave yourselves,' he snapped. We both pulled back and walked in opposite directions.

A couple of nights later I turned up at the gym as usual and the head trainer came over and warned me I'd be suspended if I was ever seen scrapping outside the ring again. I'd broken the golden rule, which was to never use the skills I'd learned inside the ring to gain an advantage in the outside world. But when you're a kid and someone starts taunting you, it's difficult not to resort to what you know best. I deserved that warning for other reasons too. I should never have let that little prat get to me. The first rule of boxing is control and I'd lost it in bucket-loads when I'd steamed into him.

Back in training at West Ham Boys' Club, older fighters continued trying to wind me up to get me to hit out at them, I only just kept my cool, and later heard that one of the trainers had put those more senior boxers up to it, just to see if I'd got the message about not losing control.

Throughout this time I kept my boxing training up to the highest standards. Sweat, leather and the slight aroma of oils they used to ease the pain of torn muscles were the overpowering smells down at West Ham Boys' Club. A typical week during school term would begin on Monday with me going out and running at least three miles as part of my boxing fitness regime. Tuesday evening, I'd pop down to the gym where I'd go through the full routine. Wednesday would be my only weekday night off, when me and my mates would go down to a youth club at Ilford Town Hall for the weekly disco. Thursday I'd be back in the club gym for training. Friday I'd always stay in and watch TV with my brothers, sister and mum. Saturday there would usually be a party at someone's house. Sunday I'd try and get to the pictures if I had any dough left on me.

My training schedule was punishing on my nights at the gym: I'd start out with the three-mile run from Forest Gate through the streets to the club. I'd have my gym bag slung over my back. It was a great way to warm up and it meant I was saving mum the cost of the bus fare.

Once in the gym, I'd head straight for the bag room where I'd spend a few minutes limbering up. The whole place was full of mirrors, which all the fighters used for shadowboxing. I'd step in front of one and start jabbing away, then would duck from side to side, using a bit of body movement, twisting and turning, keeping agile. It was all intended to get my muscles flexible and soft. I was boxing myself in that mirror. And, naturally, I always won.

Then I'd head for a sparring session. That's when it hurt the most that my old man wasn't around. Most of the kids had their dads watching and shouting for their boys. Each session, the trainer would shout orders while the fathers sat on a row of chairs up against one wall of the gym.

'Elbow in.'

'Jab straight. Don't sway.'

'Stand right.'

'Chin down.'

'Stand to the side on, *not* square.'

I could tell many of the dads felt sorry for me and I didn't like that one bit. Feeling sorry for someone doesn't help them – it just makes them even more angry. A few of the dads even hung about when I got in the ring and shouted a bit of encouragement to me because they knew my old man wasn't around. I know they meant well but it just didn't help matters. If anything it made it even more painful for me that my old man had done a runner.

I usually made mincemeat of my sparring partner and would then head off to do some skipping, back near where all the mirrors were. I loved skipping although I found it a bit tricky to start with. Once I got into the rhythm, it felt like I was floating off the floor, though sometimes I'd lose my timing and end up tangled in the rope. There's no doubt that skipping really helped my co-ordination and speed. Some trainers at the club weren't so convinced that skipping was important for a boxer, but I disagree. To achieve a double swing through one jump is quite a feat and when I started managing it, I'm sure it helped my balance inside the ring. I also got a real buzz out of achieving it.

After the skipping it would be back to some bag work. This was all about jabbing and learning. We'd use bag gloves, made out of thinner leather than normal gloves, unpadded and only 2 cm thick. They cover just the top of the hand, with black elastic on the underside, and really helped me learn how to combine punching and movement in one combination. My punches would jab twice. Then left hand, right hook, then straight punching, keeping it straight.

Then it was on to circuit training. This involved more sparring for ten minutes. The trainer either put you in with a novice or a better boy. You never ended up with someone on your own level. You always had to wear head gear with gloves, a gum shield, groin pads and boots. If you ever actually landed a proper punch the trainer would go potty, 'Come here you!' he'd yell. I got a lot of calls like that because I always wanted to beat an opponent, even if I wasn't meant to land a full-on punch on him.

I wasn't the most punch-happy boy there by any means. There were a couple of red-headed tearaways who were always trying to beat the shit out of their sparring partners. One of them once got in the ring with me and came flying at me like a bat out of hell, as if he'd just signed pro forms. He was all excited, swinging, hitting out, and he just wouldn't stop. I jabbed him off but he kept coming back for more. He was like a little Yorkshire terrier, nipping away at my ankles. Eventually the trainer jumped in and had a right go at him and he was told to go home. But I didn't have a problem with the lad because I was way out on top of him. I think the trainer was more worried I might kill the boy if he kept chasing me for a response.

Throughout these sparring sessions the trainer would keep yelling orders through the ropes:

'Move to the side.'

'Keep it tight and keep it tidy.'

'Hold your hands up.'

'Good work. Good boxing.'

You'd get a nice slap on the back if you'd done well or a nasty glare if you failed to live up to expectations.

A warm-down would follow, which was just as important as the warm-up if you wanted to avoid any nasty injuries. I'd do a load of stretches, much slower ones than for the warm-up. Then I'd take a gentle jog round a small, muddy makeshift running track in the yard behind the club.

They even had a sweat room at the club, which was often used to get a boxer to shed a few pounds to make a specific weight for a tournament. Often the boxer would have to lie in there for hours, hemmed between two smelly mattresses, sweating off as many pounds as was humanly possible. Amazingly, it was possible to lose three or four pounds in one session. But I never fancied the idea of being jammed between those two stinking mattresses.

After it was all over, I'd either allow myself the luxury of a bus ride home if I'd earlier run to the club, or I'd have to run all the way home again if I was out of dough. Each training session at the club cost a quid, which was good value when you consider it was the single most important thing in my life at that time.

During this period of my life, the old man only made occasional visits home to take us kids out for the day. He'd got himself a flashy-looking two-tone, grey and blue Ford Zephyr, with bench seats in the front that I was always sliding across whenever Dad turned a corner badly. Dad never looked scruffy. He was always well turned out and you could tell from the look on their faces that he had a way with the ladies.

Sometimes he'd take us out for pie 'n' mash. Other times he'd pop in a boozer and leave us in the car with a bottle of pop and a packet of crisps each. The keys would always be in the ignition so we could listen to the 'wireless', as he called it.

One day big bruv John, who was twelve, jumped in the driver's seat after the old man had disappeared into a boozer and drove the car across the car park, narrowly missing about half a dozen other motors. The old man was half cut by the time he came out, so he didn't even notice that his beloved car was parked up in a different place!

I also remember Dad coming round one Christmas Day so pissed that he fell asleep in an armchair. We then all chucked peanuts at him while he was kipping. We didn't exactly have much respect for him, but can you blame us?

CHAPTER THREE

# Self Defence

When I was eleven, I had my first serious boxing contest against kids from another club. We were up against Repton, the most famous club in the East End. Since my mum didn't have a car I had to get three buses to make it to their gym in Bethnal Green. And, of course, I had scruffy gear on because I couldn't afford anything special. The club only provided the gloves but I'd bought my own boxing boots from money I'd saved while cleaning cars up and down my street.

I lost that first bout to a massive lad who looked a couple of years older than me. He hit me with a flurry of punches and I struggled to keep my balance within seconds of the opening bell. I remember how everything seemed so loud in that gym. As usual, all the other kids had their dads there, shouting and urging them on and, as usual, I had no one to support me. I didn't feel too upset when I lost, but when I got home that night and my mum asked me how I'd got on, I cracked up. I went to my bedroom and sobbed my eyes out. But I wasn't going to give up – far from it. I threw myself into an even more intense round of training in preparation for the next boys' tournament.

Two months later I found myself waiting outside the Black Lion boozer next to the West Ham Boys' Club at 9 am on a Saturday morning. Minibuses and parents' cars took us to a tournament this time. As before, Mum scraped together the £2 match fee, but it meant I had to miss training a few times that week because she didn't always have the money that.

As this was a big tournament, the younger age groups went into the ring first. I had my kit on under my tracksuit so I quickly got into some warming up, shadowboxing and stretching, while the trainers taped up our hands and talked us through the coming battle.

'Remember what you've learned.'

'Keep your head, son.'

'You should be alright.'

Putting those gloves on made the butterflies start fluttering around in my tummy. Half of the adrenaline rush was caused by fear – fear of the unknown – and the other half by sheer excitement. It was an exhilarating combination.

I did a bit more shadowboxing as I waited alongside the ring. And, naturally, I tried to do it like my hero Ali. People called it showboating and, even by the age of eleven, I was the acknowledged master of it. To keep warmed up, I carried on shadowboxing until I actually entered the ring. The home fighter always got in the ring first, which was part of the tradition of the game.

Finally it was time for my fight. Nearby, parents from both sides cheered and jeered as I shadowboxed my way to my corner. As usual, my old man wasn't amongst them and Mum couldn't come because she had to look after my brothers and sister. Meanwhile, the trainers were yelling orders at me, which always got me even more hyped up and ready for battle. But by this stage all I could think of was how I'd be pummelling my fists into the opposition.

'Go kill him, son,' said one parent sitting nearby. I turned and tried to make out who it was, whether he was on my side or my opponent's. Later on in life I wondered why anyone would want to say such a stupid thing to a schoolboy boxer. Hardly sporting, is it?

Just then another parent yelled at the top of his voice at my opponent 'Do him, Mark.' Then the noise became a big blur. All the voices merged into one. The only sound I could hear above it all was my trainer. 'Remember what I told ya, son ...'

The ref beckoned that we boys should meet in the centre of the ring. Then he told us the rules. 'First thing, lads, I want a nice clean fight. No head butts, no biting, no elbows and keep it above the belt. Right, let's have a good bout.' Then we returned to our corners.

*Ding* went the bell and we were off.

I moved and ducked around a bit at first, just sizing up the enemy. I'm a southpaw, leading with my left side, and that makes me even harder to fight for any orthodox fighter. I was bouncing around, floating like a butterfly, Ali-style, or so I thought. Then I let my opponent come to me so I could try to take control of the centre of the ring. The idea was to let him do all the work. After all I was there to score as many points as I could and to win as quickly as possible. My trainer's words rang over and over again in my head.

'Win as quick as possible.'

*Ding, ding.* It was the end of round one.

Within moments my trainer and second were around me in my corner. They told me I was doing well. The next round was another classic standoff as me and my opponent tried to resist the temptation to charge in, and so lose control of the contest.

By round three the speed of both our punches had dropped because we were so knackered. The ref was barking out orders throughout.

'Keep it tight.'

'Watch your heads.'

'Not too close.'

That's when I found some extra energy to try one last long flurry to score points as quickly as possible. I charged in for that flurry and this time crunched into my target and felt him wobble under the power of my punches.

*Ding, ding.* It was the end of the final round. We were both sweating buckets and my head felt like a hammerhead had been smashing its nose against my temple.

That last bell left me feeling an overpowering combination of anticipation and exhaustion. The noise of the crowd became clear once again and there was relief that it was all over. I believed I'd won and, in later years, I was usually proved right. But there were times when I kept a low profile, said nothing and wondered why I'd been robbed of victory.

But the overpowering feeling this time was one of being so knackered it was impossible to speak or think. I sat there in the corner, with my chin resting on my chest, awaiting the final verdict. Then the ref grabbed my arm and yanked it into the air to show I'd won. 'Carl Merritt.'

I felt sorry for my opponent that day because I later found out the poor kid was under heavy pressure from his dad, who went everywhere with him. A few minutes later his old man reduced him to tears because he'd lost to me, even though he was fourteen at the time. It was about the only time I was glad my old man never showed up to see me fight.

It wasn't until I turned thirteen that I became virtually invincible in the ring. I won all three fights when we went up north to a boxing tournament. I was even awarded a trophy (made of plastic). It was the first thing I'd ever won in my life, and I felt really proud of it. But, once again, no one was there to see me win it.

Back at West Ham Boys' Club, I continued being shouted at for going in too hard, especially during sparring sessions. There was this one trainer who'd whack me over the head with a huge brown leather glove every time I lost my cool, which seemed to happen a lot! The tension simmering inside me seemed to be constantly about to explode. Boxing clearly hadn't calmed me down completely. There were times when I was still definitely out of control.

I remained quite a loner at school. I was big for my age, so no one tried to bully me but I didn't make friends easily. There were plenty of battles between my school, Forest Gate, where we wore green jackets and black trousers, and the kids at Stratford Secondary Modern, with their slick all-black uniform. We used to throw what we called Millwall bricks at them, that is newspapers rolled up so tightly they can really sting if thrown in the right way. One night the cozzers turned up in vans and grabbed a load of us and then hit us with our own Millwall bricks. I suppose we deserved it.

Inside school, PE teacher Mr Draper was always blowing his top at me and my mate Alex Dyer because we were always larking around with the weights in the school gym. 'I'm going to make an example of you two,' he'd often say, pulling a slipper out of his desk drawer. Then he'd bark, 'Hands on knees, sonny.' I'd see him turning towards me as he prepared to swipe me. It used to scare the life out of me and it was also very embarrassing because he did it in front of the class.

The headmaster, Mr Dipsdale, used the cane and I was regularly punished by him as well. There would often be a queue of boys waiting outside is study for a whacking It was like a conveyor belt some days.

Around this time, I started playing rugby at school. It's another very physical sport and I was soon getting in trouble for fighting during school matches. I played prop forward and, one time, I gave this kid opposite me an upper cut and knocked him out cold. I was sent off and then hauled before the headmaster and banned from playing for a month.

At school in the summer I did athletics, especially the shot put. I was also quite partial to the javelin- until the time I missed Mr Draper by inches when I launched it over his head. My favourite sport after boxing was really swimming. I loved. going to Romford Baths and Beckton Lido in the summer. But I often got into aggro there when I fought with other boys about who should be first off the diving board.

Throughout this time the boxing bug grew even stronger in me. I continued watching all the fights on telly at every opportunity. I was glued to the screen for the Mexico Olympics heavyweight boxing championships when that massive Cuban Teofilo Stevenson won it. I even got Muhammad Ali to sign a book he'd written when he made a personal appearance at a bookshop in the City of London. I waited three hours to meet him and was well chuffed when he winked at me and did a quick one-two with his fists to show who was boss. It was well wicked. My legs were like jelly for hours afterwards: I couldn't believe I'd just met my all-time hero.

Meanwhile me, my brother John and our mates continued getting up to mischief, although it was never too bad. I pinched a scooter when I was thirteen and we ended up smashing it into the doors of a garage because we didn't know how to drive it properly. We also did a spot of shoplifting at Woollies. I bought a brilliant fishing rod for next to nothing one time by swapping the price tags. Another day I managed to nick a pair of trousers by putting them over my own strides and walking out of the store.

Most Saturdays my brothers and me went to the kids' matinee at the local Odeon. I started wearing nicked Farrar slacks with new Remington shirts. But most of the time I stuck to jeans and Adidas trainers. I suppose you could call me a bit of a soul boy back in those days. At the local picture house, I eventually got barred for popping some kid who put chewing gum in my hair. So I started sneaking in through the back exit near the toilets. It was all good, clean fun.

One of my best memories of growing up was when my younger brother Ian and me went on holiday to Jersey Islands. We were taken by some rich friends of Mum's who'd taken pity on us because we still didn't have a bean to rub together. I must have been about twelve years old and I'd never been on an aeroplane before. It was fantastic to escape East London, all the domestic chores and boring old school. I felt a sense of freedom I'd never experienced before in my life. We stayed at this family's house on the island and it seemed like a palace. I even kissed a girl for the first time on that holiday. I met her on the beach and I remember her mum and dad lived nearby and had a swimming pool in their back garden. She was about a year older than me, with lovely long, golden hair and a gorgeous smile.

But nothing much had changed when we got back to Forest Gate. Poor old Mum was still struggling to make ends meet. Oh, and school was still a waste of time.

The green grass of Wanstead Flats provided the perfect extra training ground for my boxing. Me and my brother John and a couple of mates would run right round it two or three times a week because it was exactly three miles, which was what I was expected to run every day. Back in those days, the late seventies, there was a lot of racial tension round where I lived, which was something I definitely disapproved of. And sometimes it spilled over into my life.

One night on Wanstead Flats a Mark III Cortina rolled up alongside myself, a mate called Andy and my brother, and out popped a bunch of Asian blokes holding bicycle chains. They were obviously after aggro and I later heard they were known as the Chain Gang. We gave them a right pasting when they started trying to swing their chains in our direction. Cars were driving past and watching all the action but luckily no one called the law. A bunch of people out walking their dogs didn't even try to intervene. We never saw those Asian fellas again, but I heard they'd been pouncing on people in the area for months and we were the first ones to really take them on. After we'd sorted them out, we just carried on jogging.

My nickname at that time was 'Blue' because I wore all-blue boxing gear. My brother was known as 'Nelly' and then there two other mates called 'Smudger' and 'Hodge'. But I was never too keen on nicknames and so 'Blue' soon disappeared, never to be replaced by anything else.

Naturally, many of my mates at that time were into football, and the violence on the terraces at my nearest club, West Ham, was notorious. Every time you turned up for a match, there were fisticuffs. As I wasn't that interested in football, I didn't pay much attention to all the aggro, until I made a rare visit to the North Bank terraces for the Hammers' game against Chelsea and a copper got stabbed just next to me. I didn't like what I saw one bit. They just rounded on this cozzer when he tried to break up a scuffle. In. those days there was a group of West Ham soccer hooligans called the InterCity Firm, who were notorious for carrying blades. There was even a junior version known as the 'mini-ICF'.

I had run-ins with many of the junior members because I had a sideline going at the time minding kids' front doors when they had parties at home, to stop gatecrashers, The mini-ICF was always turning up on doorsteps, making out they were armed with blades and bottles. But me and my mates Smudger and Nelly sorted them out when they came looking for aggro one night. They were right nutters, but we never had any more problems with them after that tear-up. Violence seemed to underpin all aspects of my life at that time.

At home, we were now living with our latest 'new dad', a miserable bastard called Terry. One afternoon I walked in on him trying to slap my beloved mum. I ran after him into the kitchen so the arsehole went and shoved a meat pie in my face. I was mortified. I burst into tears and ran out of the door. My mum was shouting at me to come back but I just kept going. I didn't even have any shoes on but didn't once look back.

All my feelings of grief, loss, relief, guilt, anger and helplessness came out as I pounded the pavement through the driving rain that miserable day. I ran straight through puddles without even hesitating. I shed tears, torn by the sadness of not having a father around to help and support me.

I eventually ran into West Ham Park, more than a mile from home. It was about midday and there I was, a barefooted waif charging across the park as if I had a firework up my arse. I remember it was very muddy and my feet were caked in the stuff.

I found a quiet bench, sat down and sobbed. I just wanted to get away from all the violence and unhappiness. What was it about men that made them bring violence into our home? Around this time I'd realised most of the families round our way were in just as much chaos. Poverty and domestic bliss don't exactly go hand in hand, do they?

Eventually, darkness started to fall in the park and I began shivering. What could I do? I didn't want to go back to that bastard Terry, so I stayed put. Eventually my older brother John turned up with Terry. I felt like screaming blue murder at them, but what was the point? I shrugged my shoulders and eventually walked home with them but I refused to talk to Terry, who glared at me for the entire journey. I really hated his guts. Our war was only just beginning ...

CHAPTER FOUR

# Fighting Monsters

With my nasty 'stepdad' Terry on the scene it seemed like my mum had gone from one waster to another. Dad was well upset that Terry was going out with Mum because they'd been mates since school. Terry was always tense whenever my dad turned up to see us. But when I look back on it, Terry was tense all the time. He was tall with blondish hair and a broken nose, and always looked a bit mad, if you know what I mean. He was always ducking and diving and I think that's why he flew off the handle so easily. He'd been inside, where he'd met some right hard geezers. I reckon he was watching his back because other villains were after him. Yet for all his hard ways, he wasn't much of a boozer.

Terry and I were never going to hit it off as pals so, by the time I was thirteen, my hatred for him was pretty intense, and I was quite a big lad for my age. One day he set about punching my tiny little mum yet again – and this time I really snapped. I'd just walked in from school with my brother John and we opened the door into the kitchen to find Terry lashing out. Mum was cowering beneath him. That was it: we both grabbed him and started throwing punches. But then Terry got me by the throat. I thought he was going to kill me. John smashed him over the head with a vase and he let go. That's when I completely lost it and tried to beat him to a pulp. How dare he even lay a finger on my mum? In the end, I had to be dragged off him before he was severely injured.

John and I then stormed out of the house after my mum made it clear she'd give this arsehole the benefit of the doubt. We couldn't understand why she put up with it. But there would be a lot worse to come.

I know a lot of people will think I was nothing more than a punch-happy bully, but I was far from it. I only ever got into fights as a last resort. And some of the younger kids at school even asked me to help them out if they were being bullied by older kids. I reckon you have to stand your ground in life and help others less fortunate than yourself. My mum always brought us up to respect other people's feelings. 'If they don't bother you,' she'd say, 'you leave them well alone.' As a result, me and my brothers were never involved in any school bullying or stuff like that. It just wasn't our style.

So when my older brother John had a bust-up with a kid called Robert Allen at Forest Gate High, it almost sparked World War Three. John had come home one afternoon with his face looking like the Khyber Pass. Terry went crazy because he thought John should have put up a better fight. Terry was a racist bastard and he didn't like the fact that Robert Allen

was a black kid. Later that afternoon he dragged me and John
out by our ears and forced us to go out in his motor, looking
for this kid. It was all well out of order. Terry kept ranting
and raving about how 'that black bastard should be taught
a lesson.'

We eventually spotted Allen on Wood Grange High Road.
Terry pulled his car up around the next corner and grabbed a
length of hosepipe filled with sand out of the boot. Then he
turned to John, pushed it into his hand and told him to use it
on Allen. John looked terrified but shoved the hosepipe up his
sleeve. Then he and I began walking down the street towards
this kid Allen. We knew Terry was watching us closely.

Allen turned round as he sensed we were closing in on him.
He smashed a bottle against a wall and pointed its jagged edge
at us. He knew what we were after. We wanted revenge. I started
running towards Allen but then a hand grabbed me by the
scruff of my neck and pulled me back. It was Terry, and he
insisted John should be the one to get in the first hit with his
lethal hosepipe. Terry was one sick puppy.

John looked more scared than his prey, but then he whipped
his weapon out and smacked it across Robert Allen's face,
slicing open the flesh on his cheeks and forehead. Then John
got hold of Allen's ears and started smashing his head on the
pavement over and over again. It was not a pleasant sight. And
throughout all this, that evil piece of dirt Terry was egging him
on, 'Come on. Kill the black bastard.'

But we only wanted Allen's head on a plate because he was a
school bully, nothing more, nothing less. John completely lost it
that day and continued giving Allen an almighty pasting. A
couple of women across the street began shouting at us to stop

it. Then someone else yelled: 'We've called the Old Bill.' Terry immediately screamed: 'Get in the car – quick!'

We drove off just as the cozzers came screeching around the corner. But I knew that wouldn't be the end of it. That night Terry tooled us up and warned us that Allen would most probably be back with reinforcements. He handed me a machete blade and John was given a cutlass as long as a cricket bat. Terry had his own butcher's axe. He told us to keep our weapons near us at all times. That vindictive nutter was loving every minute of it.

The following day Terry's prophecy carne true. Robert Allen turned up with his two older brothers outside our house. I was just looking out the window for the milkman when I spotted them coming up the garden path. They stopped about five yards from the front door and one of the two brothers started taunting us to come out and face them.

Just then, at least a dozen other kids wearing Forest Gate High School uniforms swarmed along the path behind them. It was a matter of now or never. We had to catch them off guard. So me, John and Terry came charging out of the front door like a herd of rhinos. Terry slammed his axe over the gate, just missing one of the brothers. 'Come here! I'm gonna cut you in half!' he yelled; and I for one believed him.

The other two brothers and those school kids took one look at my machete and John's evil-looking cutlass and turned and ran. Looking back on it now I realise that Terry didn't give a toss about us. He just got off on the violence of it all. We didn't have any problem with Robert Allen because of his colour. We just didn't like the way he was going around bullying kids at school. Terry no doubt got a kick out of having two big kids by his side armed to the teeth. I think he manipulated us that day and we followed him because we were kids, just doing what we was told.

The next day me and my brother John had to report to the headmaster. Terry said we should deny everything. But from that day on we became known as a menacing family with violence flowing through our veins, which wasn't strictly speaking true. Sure, we'd got involved in one incident, but Terry had egged us on. Now me and John were known as nasty pieces of work. Other kids at school didn't have the bottle to talk to us, which made us both feel even more isolated. That attitude undoubtedly caused me a lot of problems later in life.

Around this time I got into a lucrative sideline painting walls at Liverpool Street Underground Station with my uncle Pete whenever I could bunk off school. I also worked on the dodgems at local fairgrounds. I had a bit of aggro when other kids got rude, when they saw me talking to my black mates. But I soon sorted them out.

Some people had the effrontery to call me a 'nigger-lover' behind my back but I didn't care. My black mate Robbie was known as the 'Bounty Bar Kid' because his black friends reckoned he was black on the outside and white on the inside.

We were all very shocked by the race riots in Brixton later, which was all over the TV news for days, but that coverage had a nasty backlash round where I lived. I was working at the fair on Wanstead Flats at the time. Two massive black kids called Delroy and Leroy smashed up a hotdog stand and then they and a few other kids tipped it over. Suddenly there was a full-scale riot going on. The cozzers then turned up in full force and the mob – now about fifty strong – headed away from the Flats and towards the Forest Gate shopping area. There, they smashed shop windows and looted TVs and stuff before heading for another shopping area called Green Street. It was bedlam. Truth was that both white and black kids joined in together and used it as an excuse to go on the rampage and nick a few things. It was completely out of order.

Just before I turned fourteen, I fell for a pretty young neighbour called Tracy, who was two years older than me. I really thought this was it and I'd spend the rest of my life with her. Then I stupidly went and got her pregnant. She was going to boarding school and her stepdad and mum insisted she was taken away and 'seen to' so the pregnancy could be terminated. I'll never forget the day I went to Plaistow Hospital by taxi to pick Tracy up. Naturally she was very upset and I tried everything to comfort her but it wasn't easy. I grew up a lot on that day.

My mum was fantastic and made a real point of looking after Tracy, as we were both too young to take on the responsibility. Tracey was getting on so badly with her family she came and lived with us for some time. We carried on going out together for three or four months after she had the abortion but it was never the same again.

At fourteen, I really thought boxing held the key to my future. I was doing well in the ring and could pack a mean punch. The trainers at West Ham Boys' Club all reckoned I'd go far and the idea of using my fists to fight my way out of the poverty trap really appealed to me. Even back then I felt a responsibility towards my mum, brothers and sister. I wanted to do good by them. I wanted them to be proud of me. One day, just before Christmas in 1979 I went down to the Pigeons pub near our home where my mum worked most nights as a barmaid. Back in those days, kids weren't allowed in boozers, but the manager let me in because I didn't drink and I loved playing pool,

That day I had a winning run at the pool table and beat this other boy, aged about seventeen, three games on the trot. He looked really narked off by the end of the third game. His mates were also taking the piss out of him for losing to a younger kid.

A few minutes later I waved goodbye to Mum, who was behind the bar and walked out of the Pigeons. As I stepped onto the pavement, an iron bar smashed right into the side of my head. I could feel my cheekbone cave in. Then the iron bar came back at me again, this time catching my jaw with an almighty crunch. I must have blacked out then because the next thing I remember is being in the back of the pub manager's car as he drove me to St Mary's Hospital in Stratford.

I was in a bad way. They had to wire up my jaw and completely rebuild my face using specialised plastic. It looked like the side of my head had been used for target practice at a golf driving range. I told the doctors in the hospital that I didn't want the cozzers involved. I ended up in there for four days and doctors informed me I'd be drinking through a straw for at least a month.

But that was nothing compared to the stress I felt about the threat to my boxing career. The doctors refused to commit on whether I'd be able to get in a boxing ring again, so I went to see my trainer down at West Ham Boys' Club. He told me there was no way I'd ever be passed fit enough by a boxing board medical to fight again because of the plastic plate they'd fitted in the side of my face. After I left the gym that day, I cried. I felt as if my life was effectively over. What future did I have if I couldn't fight in the ring?

My mum broke down when I told her the news. She knew how important boxing was to me. It was the one thing I was any good at. It was the one thing that might have helped improve all our lives. Within a week I found out where that bastard who attacked me lived, and started planning my revenge. My jaw was still bound up and I was hobbling on crutches, but none of that put me off. The manager of the pub went with me and even offered to do it for me, but I knew I had to do it myself, otherwise I'd never exorcise those demons.

I had no second thoughts. I remember almost slipping on the icy pavement as I struggled up the garden path to his maisonette. I knocked hard and firm on the front door. This was it. I wanted to hurt him as much as he'd hurt me. To be honest about it, at that moment I wanted to kill him.

The stupid bastard didn't even recognise me when he opened the door. But he certainly recognised the baseball bat that sank into his skull. 'Leave it out!' he screamed as the second and third blows came raining down on him. 'Why are you doin' this?' he asked after the next thud. For a moment I thought maybe I'd got the wrong man, but then I recognised the same orange t-shirt he'd had on when I'd beaten him at pool. As I looked down at his crumpled body on the doorstep, I spat on him. Now it was time to get on with the rest of my life.

My attacker moved house shortly afterwards and the attack was reported in the local paper. It referred to a 'mystery doorstep attack'. There was even a photo of the victim. His face looked like it had just been through a mincing machine. The paper said it was a mugging, but that was rubbish since nothing had been taken from him.

Up until that incident I'd always been on the edge, but at least I was a reasonably content sort of kid who kept his head down and got on with his boxing. All that changed after the attack with the iron bar. I didn't like anybody any more. I didn't trust a soul apart from my mum, brothers and sister.

The next couple of months were a living hell as I hobbled around home and school trying to pick up the pieces of my life, still harbouring a deep resentment. The elation I'd felt at getting revenge on that other boy had soon worn off. It was a lesson I learned about revenge: it may seem sweet at the time, but it doesn't solve any problems in the long term. I lost a lot of weight and stopped going to the gym because I couldn't see the point any more. My mum tried to pamper me to make up for what had happened. But I still presumed everyone was a threat to me apart from my family and was determined always to get the first punch in if it ever came down to a tear-up.

I still get nightmares about what happened to me at the Pigeons that night. Sometimes I'm outside my attacker's front door and he's fighting back. I can feel the pain that he caused me, even in my dream. Often, I wake up to feel if I really am injured, and there it is, this hated piece of plastic that changed the .whole course of my life. In another nightmare my assailant swings the iron bar over and over my head and I slowly sink into the ground, until there is nothing left.

With little for me to do, combined with my total bitterness towards authority and society in general, my mind started wandering towards the inevitable: crime. My first real excursion into thieving came when I was fifteen and got chatting in a pub one night with an older boy called Joe, who must have been about eighteen. He was a slim, wiry bloke who looked a bit like the pop singer Leo Sayer. Joe told me there was some real money to be earned from robbing shops, so a few days later we broke into a local Fine Fare supermarket late at night. I stayed on the roof while he slid down into the shop on a rope ladder. Then he passed all the gear up to me before we scarpered. It seemed a piece of cake and he bunged me £20 for my troubles, which was huge money back in those days.

On the next job we had to rip an alarm out from a wall above a shop before we could get in. Unfortunately, as it fell, it smashed so hard into my face it broke my nose. Joe took me down the local hospital to get my nose sorted out and then we both returned later that night to finish the job. Again, he bunged me another score – £20 – for my troubles. I felt I was rolling in it.

Then Joe suggested we do some 'pirate work' down at Leigh-on-Sea, near Southend. I didn't know what he meant but I tagged along in the hope of making a few bob to help my family. Joe nicked a rusty orange Cortina in Stratford and we headed down to the coast. Then we found a dinghy on the beach and rowed out to where dozens of boats were moored. It was pitch dark and I fell in the icy water trying to get onto one boat. But we still managed to nick a load of booze and portable TVs and stuff like that. This time Joe bunged me £50 after he'd sold off the gear to a local fence.

Funny thing about Joe was that he must have had a criminal record but he never even bothered wearing gloves. We must've been mad to think we could get away with it. He gambled a lot and told me that one night he'd blown £5000. I'm not a great one for gambling so found it hard to understand why anyone would want to waste his money like that.

Then my criminal career was rudely interrupted by the person I hated most in life.

I'd just returned from one of my regular excursions to Leigh-on-Sea when I walked into our house to find that bastard Terry at it again. Mum's face was all blown up like a football and the moment I saw it I knew he'd been smashing her up again. Without saying a word, I whacked him straight in the face and then followed up with a flurry of right hooks. Mum did nothing to stop me this time. We both knew it was time to finish off this arsehole for good.

I was a lot bigger this time compared to when we'd last had a stand-up, and I still had all that pent-up anger from getting my boxing career ruined by the iron bar. As me and Terry were scrapping, I grabbed a pen and stuck it right in his kidneys. I didn't mean to do it: it was just a defensive reaction. Terry collapsed in agony. Minutes later he crawled out of the house for the last time.

I could feel the plastic in the side of my head aching from where he'd landed a few direct hits but it was worth the pain to have taught that shit a lesson. Less than an hour later, the cozzers came knocking at our front door and said Terry had lodged a complaint against me and my older brother John, who hadn't even done anything. I couldn't believe it. That slimy bastard had not only taken a pop at my poor little defenceless mum but he'd gone and grassed us up to the law. The police wanted to take me and John down to the nick. Well, I wouldn't have any of that so I put my hand up and said I'd done all the fighting so they wouldn't nick John.

I spent that night in a cell at Forest Gate Police Station. Terry pressed for me to be charged with Grievous Bodily Harm. He must have really hated me. I was shit scared and close to tears when they locked the door of that cell. I was suddenly all alone. I threw myself onto the half-inch-thick mattress against the wall and wondered how the hell my life could be so shitty. I cried myself to sleep that night, not because I was afraid of being in the nick but because I couldn't understand how I'd allowed things to get so out of hand. And I just didn't know how any man – even sicko Terry – could point the finger at a school kid.

Back at home my mum was in a terrible state. She was outraged that they could lock a kid up on the word of her estranged, punch-happy boyfriend. And she blamed herself for what had happened. But there's no way she could be responsible for the rantings and violence of a man like Terry. The next morning the cozzers hauled me out of the cell and I gave a statement admitting what had happened. If I hadn't stuck that pen in him then maybe I wouldn't have been so harshly treated. One of the coppers said that pen turned it from a common assault charge to Grievous Bodily Harm.

I've got to say here and now the cops were fairly decent to me. They only cuffed me when they had to and they didn't rough me up at all. Round where I lived you expected a few problems down the local nick, but this time they were as good as gold. I think they felt sorry for me because Terry was so clearly a toe-rag. But there was nothing they could do as he was insisting on pressing charges. One of the coppers pulled me aside and said he thought it was a disgrace that a big fella like Terry would press charges against a fifteen-year-old kid. He reckoned I'd severely damaged Terry's pride more than anything else.

I admitted the GBH charge so they held the trial within a couple of days of my arrest. As I had no previous convictions I thought I'd get off with something like a community ser vice order. I was – and still am – a shy sort of bloke so all those people staring at me in court made me shrink even more into myself. I even caught a glimpse of that bastard Terry smirking at me from across the courtroom. I answered all the questions with a short 'yes' or 'no' and I could tell that was narking off a lot of the officials. Then there was my mum in the public gallery, close to tears. This was her baby accused of defending her against the man she now hated more than anyone else in the world. She'd earlier even tried to press counter-charges but the police told her not to bother.

The magistrate gave me three months' youth detention. My legs wobbled for a few seconds after he said it. I couldn't quite believe my ears. Then my mum stood up and shouted at Terry: 'He's the one you should be locking up.'

I was taken away in cuffs. I was about to serve a stretch inside for defending my tiny, fragile mum against a six-foot-plus bully who'd tried to smash her to a pulp. Something wasn't right, but I was too young and too scared to say anything. My head bowed, I just took the punishment. I was numbed and resigned to what had happened. I didn't fight. I didn't try to have a bundle with the guards. I just went quietly.

Minutes later I was pushed into the back of a dark blue transit van with blacked-out windows and driven off to Her Majesty's Borstal in Rochester, Kent, which was – I would soon discover – one of the worst youth detention centres in the whole of Britain. The screws picked up three other kids on the way there. Two of them were crying throughout the journey, which didn't make things any easier. Meanwhile I sat in the back chained up like a rabid dog, trying not to look too worried. But beneath my brave exterior I was in tatters. I felt broken and wasted. And I wondered if I'd ever get my life on track again.

## CHAPTER FIVE

# Two-Way Stretch

I'd been told by some relatives before my sentencing that if I was sent down then the best way to handle it was not to talk much to other inmates. My uncle Pete said: 'Keep your head down and you'll get through it, son.'

And in some ways he was right. I quickly got myself a reputation as someone not to mess with. I was considered a big, brooding 'psycho' type who hardly uttered a word, and that suited me fine. I also made a point of keeping my eyes to myself because once you catch someone's glance inside then there's always trouble.

It might sound predictable, but the most dangerous place in Rochester was the shower room. You always had to keep your wits about you and it really was a case of backs against the wall. The bullies and rapists always leered at everyone in there. They were on the lookout for the weakest. I heard one poor bastard being gang raped just a couple of cubicles from me. I couldn't do anything about it because there were four inmates standing guard while this poor little kid was abused. And it wasn't just sexual attacks in the shower room. One kid tried to stab another with an aerial he'd snapped in two and then sharpened up for an attack. Blood was everywhere as this nutter plunged his weapon into the other kid at least a dozen times. I don't know what was behind the attack, but the screws came charging in and dragged them both away. The victim's claret was still gushing down the floor drains as they rushed him to the sickbay. I later heard the attacker got a right thrashing. It was just as bad as that film *Scum*, which came out a few years back starring Ray Winstone. A lot of us called it hell.

The dorms we slept in at Rochester were pretty grim too. There were twelve kids to each room and all you had was a small bedside cabinet to put all your worldly belongings in. Naturally, anything of value was soon pinched. And there was a lot of farting and wanking going on at night, which didn't exactly add to the friendly atmosphere.

One of my next-door neighbours in that dorm was this Italian-looking kid who constantly combed his hair. He really got up my nose. He had a sly way of looking at you as he combed his hair over and over again. Eventually I couldn't stand watching him any longer so I barked at him to stop doing it or else I'd have to sort him out. He nodded his head, stopped and moved away. Then he started up again in the other corner of the dorm.

We each had a single bed and lights went out at 9 pm. Some of the kids were such basket cases they cried themselves to sleep which made it bloody depressing. A lot of them were burglars while a handful were in for violence, including me. That's why most of the other kids left me alone.

Most of us had a picture of a naked bird hanging on the wall by our bed. I also had a couple of weird faces that I'd drawn in art classes. But that Italian arsehole with the comb had photos of fighter airplanes. What a loser! One time I spotted his comb on the floor and threw it in the bin, in the hope it might stop him combing his hair all day. Bastard simply produced another one from his bedside cabinet.

The way the screws woke us up each morning at Rochester was a bloody outrage. Three of them would come in and start screaming, 'Get up, you lazy little wankers.' Then they'd start kicking the ends of our beds. Butlins it was not.

Despite that earlier advice from my relatives, I couldn't resist sometimes looking the nastiest screws straight in the eye, challenging them to have a pop at me but they didn't bother. They'd seen me in the gym and had heard the rumours about my past as a fighter.

My work duties in Rochester weren't too bad because I was assigned to the garden. But two nasty incidents happened, which luckily the screws never knew anything about. One morning I was in the gym room, on a workbench pulling weights, when this other kid marched in and said I was on his bench. I ignored him at first. Then he started really throwing his weight around so I had to give him a slap with a dumbbell. I've never forgotten how I visualised it was the face of that bloke who ruined my life after I beat him in that game of pool. This fella went down like a sack of frozen chips. I walked straight out of the gym before anyone else even noticed what had happened. Later I heard this same kid being given a grilling by a screw who wanted to know why his face was all mashed in. 'I fell over, I fell over.' He kept saying it over and over again. That's how it went inside.

A few weeks later I was working in the garden when some kid decided to crack me over the head with a shovel because he didn't like the way I was looking at him. I whacked him straight back with a flurry of rights followed by a left square on the face. The kid went flying but everyone just carried on working as if nothing had happened. A screw turned up just as this kid was getting to his feet. Just like the other kid before him, he told the officer: 'I fell over, I fell over.'

Even without these incidents, my life wasn't exactly a bed of roses inside Rochester. We had to be up at 6 am for a 6.30 am breakfast. Then it was straight off to work. I spent most of my time planting and digging up vegetables in the greenhouse. I really did try to keep my head down. I didn't want any aggro – I just wanted to get home.

The sound of my fists pounding into the heavy bag soon regularly permeated the prison gym. I usually started something like this: tap ... tap ... with my left fist. I'd push my arms away from my body, but the bag would still swing and the top links of the chain holding it to the ceiling would start grating against each other and would squeak. Then I'd pop a right into the battered brown leather. It might not have looked like a hard shot, but the heavy bag would this time jump on its little chain. Once I'd got the bag swinging, I'd begin to pound away: left, left ... and then right ... WHACK; left, left ... right ... WHACK; left, left ... right ... WHACK. Air would wheeze out of the bag with every slap, the noise from the chain punctuating my swings.

Other inmates would look on, knowing that those shots I was inflicting on the leather bag could soon be beating out a rhythm on some poor bastard's boat race or rib cage if they weren't careful.

Each time I visited that gym, I got fitter. My face became ruddy from the outdoor work, running and skipping round the Rochester yard for an hour every morning. I'd have easily ballooned up to fifteen or sixteen stone if I wasn't training, but now I was fit again, my optimum weight was around fourteen-and-a-half stone. I suppose you'd call it fighting fit.

I always trained in a T-shirt, old sweatpants and dirty white trainers, which I never bothered lacing up. Before I got sent down I'd appeared huge but shapeless – no neck, beefy shoulders, big arms and the rest coming out in all the wrong places. But being in the slammer turned me into a sculptured, toned-up master of the universe, if you know what I mean. Despite everything, I was sharper, tighter. My bulk was closing in on itself, huddling my frame. I felt compact and constantly wound up. I was on full alert.

My dear old mum came to see me once a week in Rochester. She'd always start off each visit by smiling at me and saying: 'You'll be out soon, son.' Then she'd spend the entire visit babbling on about my brothers and sister and what was happening back at home. I couldn't get a word in edgeways and I knew she was trying her hardest to avoid cracking up. I could see in her eyes that she was holding herself back from crying. Trouble was that watching her suffer made me feel like shit. It broke my heart to see her in such distress.

At the end of each visit, she'd give me a hug and I could feel her shaking like a leaf, still holding back the tears. I knew that if I hugged her too long then she'd completely crack up so I'd sort of push her away. Sometimes the bad things you do are done for a good reason. She told me later how she'd then go home and sob her eyes out. She never wanted to show me how upset she really was but I knew all along. It's typical of my mum to try and always be strong.

Meanwhile the staff at Rochester continued to prove themselves to be total wankers. If they could get one over on an inmate they would. It was all like a game to them and there were a lot more sensitive souls than me around.

There was one particularly evil screw who baited up a fight between me and a boy who was supposed to be the 'Big Daddy' inside – the kid no-one dared take on. This screw kept trying to wind us up to have a tear-up. He got his kicks from seeing this so-called tough kid bashing the shit out of other, weaker inmates. In the end, I fell for the bait and gave the so-called 'Big Daddy' the hiding of his life, which was nothing more than he deserved.

The only member of staff I even vaguely got on with was the art teacher. I did twelve hours of art a week. I couldn't get enough of it: I loved it. It was like a release from all my problems, which enabled me to escape into a fantasy world and, believe me, I needed something to help me forget my troubles.

I specialised in painting faces. They were all imaginary, well sort of. And they all looked a bit bloody miserable. Many were faces of people from my past – like that bastard who slammed an iron bar over my head at the Pigeons pub and that arsehole 'stepfather' Terry, who'd landed me in borstal in the first place.

I had a special technique when I was drawing. I'd start at an eye or the nose and then work my way out from there. I never knew what I was going to end up painting; bit like my attitude to life, I suppose. I'd just strike out with my brush or pencil and then see how the mood took me. That art teacher encouraged me a lot. He seemed to understand what was going through my head, which is more than I can say for any of the teachers back at school.

Often I'd end up with two faces looking at each other. Sometimes I even managed four faces on each page. Their haunted look reflected what I felt at the time. How could I have done pictures of smiling, happy faces if I didn't feel it myself?

I also drew cartoons – some called them caricatures – of people in the borstal. I'd pick out people's faults, like a big nose or a bulbous mouth, and make them look even worse. There were a couple of screws I loved painting in a really distorted way but I'd always tear the pictures up into pieces if any of them marched into our dormitory. Pity I couldn't do the same thing to them in real life!

There was one huge, fat bully of a screw with a goatee beard who featured over and over in my cartoons. I hated him so much, I couldn't get him out of my mind. Anyway, one time I drew a cartoon of him sitting on the toilet, looking like a big fat prat (which is what he was) and stuck it up on the wall to amuse my cellmates. I was asking for trouble but didn't give a toss. The screw walked in one day and, surprise, surprise, spotted the picture, but the funny thing is he didn't recognise the figure as himself, even though everyone else said it was a good likeness. He just snatched it off the wall and tore it into little pieces without saying a word. But news of my caricatures eventually reached the borstal's counsellors, whose job it was to assess if I was ready for release. Naturally, they believed I was still a bolshy youngster who might be a danger to society. I answered every one of their questions with 'Fine'. I didn't want to give anything away about myself. I've always been like that.

I eventually left the counsellors' office knowing they had me labelled as a nasty, violent delinquent, not prepared to face up to what I'd done. This couldn't have been further from the truth. I'd steamed into Terry to stop him battering my mum – it's as simple as that. But the authorities never looked at it from my point of view.

About a week before I was due for release I was called into the Assistant Governor's office to take an important personal phone call. It turned out to be my Uncle Pete. He said: 'You can't go back home next week, son. You gotta steer clear in case that bastard Terry comes looking for you.' I insisted I wasn't scared of Terry but Uncle Pete said the family had decided it was too dangerous for me.

So here I was, about to get out of one cage only to be dropped right into the middle of another. Story of my life, I suppose. Even after serving time for giving him the beating he deserved, the spectre of Terry was haunting me.

A week later I got out of Rochester. Me and two other kids stepped out of the gate and heard it sliding shut behind us. I thought to myself 'Well, you're on your tod now. No more nice gentle screws to tuck you up at night. Back to the real world.' I couldn't wait. I shivered, not from the cold but, as my mum would say, 'Because someone just walked over your grave, Son.'

I was five-feet-eleven-inches of pure muscle from all that time spent in the borstal gym. I'd been capable of growing a beard since the age of fourteen. I was a man in everything but actual age.

The year had started badly with that iron bar attack at the Pigeons that wrecked my boxing career, then I'd got banged up for beating up that bastard Terry. Now I was determined to start my life all over again. There was no turning back.

The few decent screws back at Rochester had told me it was the air you first noticed when you got out. 'Air doesn't have to smell of disinfectant,' they said. 'You think this is normal ... wait till you smell real air again.' At the time I hadn't given it much thought but now I was out I remembered every word.

The same dark blue transit with the blacked-out windows that had delivered me to the hell hole was waiting to take us boys back to East London. No one said much in the van as we drove through Kent and then into the Dartford Tunnel. The bright florescent lighting in the tunnel made me squint. I was so relieved when we finally drove up into the grim grey of the East End. The screws pushed us out just by Bow Station.

Over to one side, near where the steps led up from Bow Underground Station, an old boy in a brown plastic apron was opening up a flower stall. As the van pulled away, I strolled over to him but he ignored me.

'Got any daffs?' I asked him.

'Over there.'

They were at the far end of the stall, high up at the back. I reached across and took down a bunch. They were still wet, and bound tightly together with elastic bands.

'Fifty pence,' the old boy said.

I fingered the coins: some of them had been taken off me when I'd been nicked. I was just about to hand over the money when I heard my name being called. I turned round to see Uncle Pete and two of his heavyweight mates in a white Cortina. Uncle Pete looks a lot like my dad. He's four years younger, a big rock-' n' -roller and six feet tall. Still works out every day.

'Forget the flowers, Son,' he said in his strong East End twang. 'You're comin' home with me.'

I certainly wasn't going to have a ruck with him so I jumped in the back of his Dagenham Dustbin.

While we drove across London to Pete's home in Croydon, South London, he and his mates talked about the doorman game and how someone with my skills would fit in perfectly. Uncle Pete had been running a crew of doormen for a few years down at some nightclubs in Croydon.

That night I kipped at Uncle Pete and Aunt Marge's house. 'You're here till further notice, Son,' he said. I knew I was going to enjoy myself and, to be honest about it, I knew I needed a fresh start. Maybe this cage wasn't going to be so bad after all.

A couple of nights later, me, my mum and brothers John and Ian steamed into a few bevvies at Uncle Pete's local boozer. Ian and John ended up having to carry Mum and me back to Pete's house but no one was complaining. After what we'd been through, a few drinks were perfectly natural.

I had a nasty dream that night about being attacked in borstal and I was sweating heavily when I opened my eyes and saw the sun peeping through the window. I suppose I still expected some lousy screw to waltz in and start barking orders at me and kick the shit out of the end of my bed.

I'd survived all those months in borstal without even touching a ciggie but the deadly weed went and hooked me within days of getting out. And life inside Rochester had made me grow up quickly. I'd probably seen more than most blokes twice my age. But I knew I now had to do something with my life. It wasn't going to be easy. There'd been too many knockdowns already and I didn't honestly know if I was up to the challenge.

I jumped at the chance of working the door at a club with Uncle Pete and his crew because I desperately needed to start earning a wedge. Mum turned a blind eye to the fact I was missing school – she just wanted me off the streets, where I might get up to no good. I assured Pete I was fighting fit and ready for work. I was fifteen and about to get a taste of the real world.

## CHAPTER SIX

# Money in my Pocket

I always reckoned that not much of the old man ever rubbed off on me, but now I know that's not completely true. He was always a diplomat if ever there was any aggro. He never just steamed in and caused trouble. He liked to talk about things first and then, if someone ignored him, *whack,* he'd go in with all fists blazing. His brother – my Uncle Peter – was the opposite. He always told me: 'Don't give up. Don't lose. You ain't gonna lose as long as you think you ain't gonna lose.' Uncle Pete certainly wasn't shy about knocking a few heads together if he felt the need. He went in hard and fast and took no prisoners.

It was Uncle Pete who really taught me much of what I know today. He taught me self-respect and he also showed me the importance of manners. Not having my dad at home meant that was doubly important. And Uncle Pete was certainly quite a character. He was so into heavy rock that he used to drag me to pop concerts in fields and events like that. He especially loved the Eagles and the Rolling Stones.

My first door job with Uncle Pete was at a Croydon night-club called Scamps. Me and all the other doormen had to wear a red shirt, black bowtie (clip-on, naturally) and a black jacket. I was still just fifteen years old, but no one back at school in Forest Gate even bothered to come after me. I already weighed in at nearly fifteen stone with a seventeen-inch neck and well-toned biceps to match. No one there (apart from Uncle Pete) had a clue how young I was. If they had, then I'd probably have had a lot more trouble with the customers.

But it didn't take more than a few days on the door at Scamps for some aggro to flare up. 'Get your arse down here,' screamed Uncle Pete over the walkie-talkie, seconds after a punter outside the club had tried to smash a bottle over his head. I sorted out the assailant and we made sure he never came back to Scamps again.

I worked three full nights a week at Scamps and stood in for many of the other doormen if they were off sick. There were seven doormen in total working at the club at any one time. One night a few weeks after I'd started, I was walking up the stairs to the club entrance when a familiar-looking figure walked down the other way, right past me. I blinked twice to make sure I wasn't seeing things. It was my dad. I hadn't seen him in years.

He turned back. 'Heard you was here,' he said to me as our eyes met. I was well annoyed to find I was working at the same club as the old man, who had worked as a doorman at loads of clubs over the years. I suppose I should have known better since it was his brother Pete who was running the door. But I still couldn't get that clash between him and my mum out of my mind. I knew he'd been given quite an ear-bashing by my mum, but nothing gave him the excuse for tearing into her the way he did.

I said nothing at first and just gave him a kind of steely look, right into his eyes. I suppose I was waiting for him to say sorry for fucking up the lives of his four kids and wife. But instead he just grinned at me as if nothing was the matter. That really grated with me at the time. I wanted him to grovel for what he'd done to us.

'Ain't you even goin' to say hello to your old man?' he said, trying desperately to break the ice.

'Fuck off,' I said, surprised at my own coldness.

Just then Uncle Peter appeared on the stairs. He must have sensed the tension in the air because he immediately tried to calm things down by proudly telling my old man about how I'd handled myself during that tear-up a couple of days earlier.

Pete laughed and joked as he described how I'd steamed in and sorted it all out. Just then a smile came to my old man's lips and I decided to give him the benefit of the doubt. Maybe he wasn't really so bad after all. We'd get along fine just so long as we both realised where to draw the line.

Not long after starting on the door at Scamps I got my first taste of the rivalry that exists between firms of doormen across London. A mob from a club on the other side of Croydon had decided to try and take over Uncle Pete's doorman contract at Scamps.

At first the rival firm put the word around Croydon that Pete and his crew were no better than a bunch of schoolgirls and that they were the real men for the job. Basically, they were throwing down the gauntlet to us. They wanted our business and that's not something any doorman will give away without a real battle.

Uncle Pete and the rest of us soon heard about these prats so a meeting was organised in the car park out the back of Scamps. It was scheduled for early Saturday evening before the club opened for business.

What followed was more like a scene out of the Wild West than south London. Pete got us all assembled out the back of the club to await our 'guests'. Eventually two BMWs and a Merc turned up in the club car park and out jumped our heavyweight rivals.

Their leader – a short stocky fella with a bald head and moustache – was obviously itching for a tear-up. 'How d' you want to do this?' he asked Uncle Pete. 'Hands or tools?'

'Hands,' Pete snapped back. We knew we wouldn't need weapons to show them who was top dog.

Pete had earlier briefed us that the moment he responded was the signal for the tear-up to start. We had been told to select ourselves an individual target and steam straight in.

I went for the bloke who happened to be the nearest and was soon swinging my fists right in his face before following through with some vicious kicks to his stomach and thighs. He was in his late twenties and all bulked up like Arnie in *Terminator*. But I didn't give a toss, I had no fear. I suppose part of the reason was that I'd turned sixteen years old the previous day. Fear just wasn't something I understood or appreciated.

Anyway, as it happens, it turned into a right old-fashioned tear-up – and thank God there wasn't a blade in sight! They had about ten geezers on their side – three more than us so we should have been odds on for a hiding, but it didn't quite work out according to their plan.

I finished my first victim off by catching him with a straight left to the adam's apple. He went down like a bag of cement. Then I jumped on the back of another fella who was handing out a right pasting to Uncle Pete. Across the other side of the car park, my old man was giving rock-all to some fat old bear.

As I swung around on the back of the Giant Haystacks lookalike, I could hear the dense rat-tat-tat sound as the crack of punches connected with their targets across the car park. I could taste blood in the back of my throat.

I got my latest target to the floor and started whacking him hard in the back of his neck. He crumbled like a meat loaf. Meanwhile Pete had switched his battle to the guv'nor of the opposition. He definitely had the upper hand and seemed to be finishing off this other bloke. Across the way my old man had moved onto a new target and was hammering away at some poor bastard who looked as if he was about to collapse on the tarmac.

Suddenly Dad looked up. 'It's done. It's done,' he yelled ecstatically. All around us were the moaning and groaning remains of this rival firm who'd decided we were ripe for a takeover bid. They retreated so quickly, they left behind two of their soldiers unconscious on the floor. One of them was out cold and the other was moaning like an elephant. Their mates had screeched off in their flashy motors. The entire fight had lasted no more than five or six minutes.

We marched off towards the back entrance of the club just as sirens could be heard in the distance. The two injured doormen helped each other to their feet and scrambled off into the Saturday evening crowds of shoppers. The cozzers turned up to find the whole car park swimming in claret but little else. They knew what had happened but without any bodies there wasn't much point in pursuing the matter.

Once we were inside the club, Uncle Pete came up to me and slapped me on my back. 'You done good, Son. You done good,' he said. I felt immensely proud. 'There aren't many who stand their ground. But you certainly did,' added Pete.

Later that night Uncle Pete warned both me and my old man that the opposition might come back for a return grudge match and we were told to keep a close eye on things for the next couple of weeks. But nothing ever came of it, although from that day on Uncle Pete made sure we were always tooled up with coshes, dusters and baseball bats hidden in strategic positions around the club.

Although I didn't realise it at the time, Uncle Pete had watched me closely during that tear-up in the Scamps car park. He'd earmarked me for bigger things.

About a week after that clash with the rival firm of doormen, Uncle Pete took me to see a local prize fight between two doormen from the Croydon area. It was to be held behind the closed doors of another local nightclub called Lacey Lady's. The two fighters used extra-heavy gloves, which looked almost comical because they were twice the size of normal boxing gloves.

The prize money was X400 for the winner and £200 for the loser. It was a bit of a joke, really. The audience was encouraged to have a pop at the last winner and half of them were so tanked up they could hardly see their way into the ring. And most of them looked like fat, unfit slobs to me. The so-called 'champ' was pretty trim and bouncy. Watching those stupid punters having a go at him was pathetic. It seemed like easy money to me.

I found it fascinating to watch, and reckoned I could see off most of those characters with a swift flurry of punches. I boasted to Uncle Pete that I was better than any of them. He laughed when I first said it but then I got serious.

'You really up for it?' Pete asked me. 'Why not?' I said.

I'd just turned sixteen years old but I had no fear of anyone. In fact I reckoned I could show most of them a thing or two about the fight game. They'd be like lambs to the slaughter.

CHAPTER SEVEN

# Man on a Mission

I couldn't get that prize fight at Lacey Lady's out of my mind. Uncle Pete made a point afterwards of asking me what I thought of the whole scene. I just shrugged my shoulders, smiled and said to him, 'Looks like a piece of piss to me. They're weren't up for much were they?' Uncle Pete smiled back and laughed, 'I reckon you mean that, Son. Well, your time will come. Your time will come.'

I didn't sleep much that night because I kept thinking over and over what I'd have done if I'd got in the ring with those drunken old slobs. A few days later Uncle Pete asked me if I wanted to go to another fight challenge later that week at the same club. I had my suspicions about Pete's motives, but it didn't bother me that he might be planning to send me in the ring. Pete then told me he'd had a word with the management and they'd agreed that I could go in the ring and have a dig at a few of the old timers. No one other than Uncle Pete had any idea I was just sixteen years old.

'When you get in there, just get it done quick as poss,' said Pete. I couldn't wait to get back in the ring and feel that leather on my fists, even if it was going to be the sort of contest that boxing purists would have hated. Uncle Pete even warned me: 'Some of them'll be a bit dirty with the elbows and heads.' But I already knew all that after a good few street fights and that recent tear-up with those rival doormen in the Scamps car park.

The night before my first appearance in an unlicensed ring, I played table-tennis with Uncle Pete and a few of his mates who'd popped into his house in Croydon for a few jars. Some of them thought it was a right laugh that Pete was putting me up for a fight the next day.

'Let's hope you get a drunk,' said one of them, a skinny old survivor called Tel.

'Yeah, one puff and he'll fall over,' chipped in another mate of Pete's called Reg.

I looked seriously at both of them because I was after more of a challenge than just a fat drunk. 'I'd like someone a bit tastier,' I said in the sort of solemn tone that all sixteen-year-olds specialise in. I could tell from the look on most of their faces that they thought I was some daft kid heading for the thrashing of my life.

We all had a few beers and a laugh that night, although I was careful not to drink or eat too much because I wanted to be in prime condition for the next day. I'd been keeping fit ever since that spell in borstal but I hadn't been near a punch bag in ages. My main exercise had been four-mile runs across the

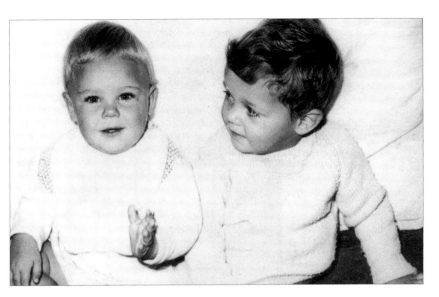

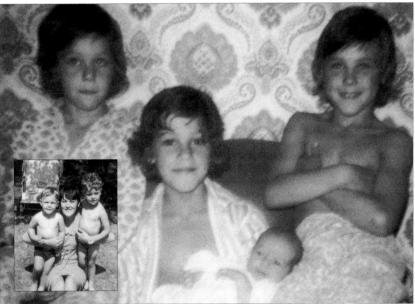

*Top*: Me and my big brother John. I was a bit of a blond bombshell in those days!

*Bottom*: (*from left to right*) Ian, John and me with baby sis Lee, just a few days after she popped out into this big, bad world.

*Inset*: Me with John and our mum on a rare day out at the seaside.

*Top*: Here's a rare snap of my dad and mum together, before the demons set in.

*Right*: This is me in one of my favourite New Romantic poses back in the Eighties, complete with a blond streak or two in my hair!

*Top*: Me and Carole when we were courting. She's the most beautiful girl in the world and the best thing that ever happened to me.

*Middle left*: Me and my brother John dancing at the wedding... What a bash!

*Below left*: Our big wedding with (*from left to right*) dad, pageboy Christopher, bridesmaid Kelly, my dear old mum, big brother John, me and my wonderful Carole, sister Lee, Carole's mum Brenda and her dad Jim.

Mean, moody and fighting fit – it was me against the world and I'd do anything to protect my family.

In the cage the only weapons you have are your fists, elbows, feet, teeth and forehead. It's the deadliest sport there is, and there's no escape: it's them or you.

*Top*: Me and Carole during that first trip to Los Angeles, where I ended up fighting in a cage built in a car park near the airport.

*Above*: Soaking up the sights after landing in Sydney, where we were hoping for a new life.

*Right*: Me in Melbourne just before I took on a mad and dangerous Aussie, and only just escaped with my life.

*Top*: Me with my lovely daughter Melanie in California, just before that final Las Vegas fight that truly changed my life.

*Above*: Me with some of the gang on the Michael Caine flick, *Shiner*, on which I worked as a fight advisor.

*Left*: With two of the most important people in my life: baby Jaime (*left*) and Melanie.

The cage was a serious business but now I'm out of that game for ever, life just gets better and better.

fields around the old Croydon Airport near where Uncle Pete lived. Usually I had his two Rottweilers, Pinky and Perky, for company.

Next morning I was up at dawn, doing press-ups and shadow boxing in my tiny bedroom at Pete's house. After running out over the fields with Pinky and Perky, I arrived back at Uncle Pete's and demolished a bowl of cereal and three slices of lightly buttered toast. The old butterflies were flapping around inside me by now. The countdown had begun. I glanced up at the clock. It was about nine o'clock. In six hours I'd be in there hammering some poor bastard into a piece of pulp. I couldn't wait. All that pent-up fury for that arsehole who'd finished off my boxing career and that nasty bastard Terry was building up yet again. I could feel a twisted knot inside me stretching itself to breaking point. I hardly said a word to Pete or Aunt Marge that morning. My mind was totally immersed in what I was about to do. Pete knew it and left me in peace.

About mid-morning, Uncle Pete, me and all his boys from Scamps met up at a small boozer just a short walls from Lacey Lady's club, the venue of my prize-fighting debut. It was jam-packed with the sort of people I expected to see later at the fight. And there in the corner, supping his customary pint of Guinness, was my old man. He looked half pissed already, but I suppose I was kind of happy he was there. He was full of it, naturally. You'd never have guessed he'd hardly seen me since I was knee-high. 'Can't wait to see my boy get in there and fuckin' crush 'em to pieces,' he said to anyone who'd listen.

I sipped slowly on a flat orange juice; nothing fizzy in case I got hit in the gut, as then I'd bring it all back up. The old man continued rambling on. 'Just remember, Son, fast flurries of punches in the gut and they'll fuckin' crumble ...' I nodded but found it difficult to look him in the eye. His words were more of a performance for other punters than a sincere piece of advice from a father to his son.

So I sat there and let all the rest of them do the talking. About two dozen blokes came up and slapped me on the back and wished me luck. To tell you the truth, I got sick of hearing them very quickly. All I wanted to do was get in that ring.

At one stage I looked over at Uncle Pete and caught a glance from him that told me he knew what was going through my mind. 'Come on, Son. let's get movin,' Pete finally said, jumping to his feet. At last the time was approaching.

Me and Pete, plus my old man and about eight of their mates, got up and headed for the door. We walked down Croydon High Street. It was peak shopping time on a Saturday afternoon and the crowds were out in full force. But the sight of us must have freaked a few of them out because most people drew aside for us like the Red Sea. I remember we passed a couple of young tearaways. They looked us up and down, and must have wondered what the hell we were up to. After all, you don't often get a dozen meaty characters out on their own on a Saturday afternoon, do you?

We were all laughing and joking on the way. One of Uncle Pete's best mates chipped at me: 'I might have a go later myself, Carl.' But I knew he didn't mean it. Whenever a pretty bird walked by, some of the older fellas would blow a long wolf whistle. 'Look at the bristols on that one.' 'What a cracker.' That sort of stuff. But my mind remained on other things.

We must have looked terrifying; all in tight T-shirts with biceps bulging. I spotted a couple of coppers on the beat, walking down the road from us. As soon as they saw our mob they ducked down a side road: we were that scary. And having all these heavies around me helped make me feel even more confident for the fight. I felt invincible. I suppose that's why they make such a production of every fighter's entrance to a big contest. But instead of Wembley or Earl's Court I had Croydon High Street!

Eventually we got to the car park of Lacey Lady's and I warmed up with Uncle Pete at my side. The others – including the old man – went ahead of us into the club. I found a quiet corner of the car park well away from the club and, shielded by a high-sided white transit, started doing press-ups and sit-ups on the tarmac. I didn't want any of the opposition to spot me. Mind you, I don't think any of them had even considered a proper pre-contest warm-up. As this wasn't a real boxing match, I was wearing jeans, trainers and a tight white T-shirt. That way if the place got raided, the Old Bill couldn't accuse anyone of running an illegal prize fight.

I carried on my own circuit of training behind that van until Pete whistled across and beckoned me to follow him. As we walked in, he nodded at the club doormen and a few of them gave me an up-and-downer. Inside, we walked through a long corridor towards the main bar area.

There was a slight hush amongst the punters as me and Pete walked into the main bar area. Pete gave the manager a nod. I turned round and spotted two gorgeous strippers doing their thing on a couple of small circular stages off in the corner of the main area. They looked a scrumptious sight to a sixteen-year-old kid.

'Want a bevvy, Son?' asked a voice.

I shook my head and carried on looking at those birds. I wouldn't touch a drop of the hard stuff until I'd completed my mission, so to speak. And you gotta remember, I was still incredibly angry about how my boxing career had gone down the pan. Nothing was going to divert me from the job at hand.

A Duran Duran song was playing in the background and those girls were snaking their hips like Pan's People. Lacey's even had one of those shiny disco balls going round and round, hanging off the ceiling. The whole event looked and felt like a cross between *Rocky* and *Saturday Night Fever.* Then Pete snapped me out of my ogling trance by tapping me on the shoulder to ask if I wanted an orange juice.

There were mirrors on virtually every wall and at least a dozen blokes were shadow boxing in time to the music. Then I spotted the ring itself across the bar-room area. It had four posts with canvas-floor decking and three layers of rope, but it definitely looked smaller than the average ring, which meant I'd have to be double quick at finishing off the opposition. I didn't want to give them any time to recover. Pete told me they made it smaller to ensure there wasn't too much chasing around the ring. The crowd wanted hand-to-hand action, none of that fancy footwork that I used to pride myself on.

There were three or four doormen types inside the ring, plus what looked like the club manager in a black suit and a dicky-bow. But for the moment I remained more interested in ogling the strippers – they were out of this world! One was blonde and the other brunette and they had tassels on their nipples, which they were somehow managing to swing around as they danced. I was mesmerized.

Behind me more and more blokes were pouring into the club.

I finally took my eyes off the strippers when a voice barked over the PA system, 'If you want a fight put your name down now.' I glanced across and saw a pad of paper sitting on the bar. Then me and Pete pushed through the crowd and got to it.

There was only one name ahead of me on the list. I was a bit disappointed because I wanted to take on a lot more than just one old drunk. 'Come on. Sign this,' said Uncle Pete. 'There'll be a bunch more later, once the booze has kicked in,' he added, reading my mind as usual.

It was only then that it really hit me that I was about to get in that shabby-looking ring and have a pop at someone. A few minutes later I had another glance at the book and two more names had been added. 'Told you,' said Uncle Pete.

Then he nodded at me to follow him over towards the ring area. The atmosphere was really warming up. There was an expectant buzz in the air. And a lot of laughing and joking among the audience. I saw a few of them slapping huge wads of cash into the club manager's palm. He had a leather bag under his arm and then pulled out a notebook and wrote down each bet. My Uncle Pete stopped and walked over to the manager and handed him a crisp new banknote. 'Put a score on my boy Carl,' he said.

As we continued across the room, Pete told me that two of the fighters had previously performed at the club and were fairly well known. 'But that doesn't mean they're up to much,' he said. I noticed the club manager was still writing down bets and then ripping slips of paper out of his notebook and giving them to punters.

'Put yer money on him,' said one voice as I walked past. 'He looks a fuck sight tastier than the rest of them.'

I was as quiet as a mouse by this stage, leaving all the talking to Uncle Pete, who seemed to know just about everyone in Lacey Lady's that day. Then my eyes panned the audience and the rest of the room to see if I could spot any of the other fighters.

Just then my dad appeared alongside us and pointed at a man in his early forties whose nose was seriously squashed to one side: 'That's one of them,' he said. This character's eyebrows were sunken in the way many old pros suffer once they reach middle age. I also couldn't help noticing a big beer belly. But there was something about him that put me on edge and I hoped I didn't get him first. Then my dad chipped in again and explained he was an ex-doorman who'd been a prize fighter for years.

'But he's pretty harmless, Son,' he added before looking across at another younger bloke standing near to us. 'Now that's the fella you want to worry about,' said my dad. This one looked tall and slim but so pissed out of his head, he was swaying in the wind. He certainly didn't look like a bruiser. He was too clean cut. Maybe the old man was winding me up. Then he said, 'He's a gym instructor and he's well sharp. Don't be fooled by the state of him. He's fast and fit, which is a lot more than can be said for most of these sad bastards.' I wondered if the old man was including himself.

The third fighter pointed out to me was an unknown punter. Maybe he was the danger man, I thought to myself. Maybe this wasn't going to be so easy after all.

A few minutes later, the first fight got under way. It was the old boy with the beer gut versus the mystery punter, a stocky, ex-squaddie-looking type. The ref was the same club manager who'd been taking all the bets. He barked out a few orders and then leaned in towards the mystery punter waiting in his corner. 'What's your name, Son?'

I couldn't hear the reply, but suddenly the ref pops his head up and screams: 'Jim Phelan versus one of our best known regulars, Frank Page.' By now they've got these huge gloves on. They look comical because the gloves are so much bigger than standard fight gloves. Bit like something out of Tom and Jerry.

The ref then screams at them: 'Now remember, lads. No headbutting. No biting. No kicking. And lads, don't take it too fuckin' serious.' He drops his hand and they're off.

The rest of us had taken our places at dozens of tables and chairs spread out around the ring area. I was seated with Uncle Pete, my dad and a couple of their cronies, all of whom were doormen. They were shouting and screaming abuse at both fighters, accusing them of being a pair of right wankers.

I kept my mouth shut and studied every move really closely but the fight didn't last long. The old boy with the beer gut might have been out of condition but he knew how to get himself into a right frenzy and he was sending in flurry after flurry of sharp, heavy punches. The other geezer had no way of handling it. He tried to hit back but didn't even have the reach to connect any of his own punches, even though they were both a similar height. The old boy had a lot more weight on him, and his opponent had made the mistake of not taking him seriously. I learned a quick lesson watching them scrapping: never underestimate your opponent. Even if he looks like he's wasted, be careful.

Just then the old boy steams in with yet another flurry of master-strokes and the punter crumbles to the deck. The ref leaps in and puts his hand up to end it. 'Well done, lads. Now shake on it.'

It looked ridiculous when the winner tried to shake his opponent's hand because the other man was still lying groaning on the floor at the time.

Uncle Pete and my old man were laughing and clapping both fighters. 'I reckon I could 'ave him easy,' my dad yelled over to his brother. I looked across at Uncle Pete and he winked. He knew what I thought of the old man. In any case, there was no way my dad was going to grab my glory that night. And I knew from Pete's reaction he was thinking along the same lines.

A short interval followed that first bout so that everyone could top up their glasses. That's when the club manager went over and had another look at the pad to see who was next up for a scrap. My eyes had wandered back to the strippers by this time. They looked as tasty as ever.

Suddenly there was a tap on my shoulder. It was the club manager. 'You're next, Carl,' he screamed in my ear. 'You're fightin' that guy, Adam.' He then pointed at the gym instructor two tables away who was just standing up. 'Go get your gloves on, Son.'

Adam saw us pointing in his direction. He nodded and winked at me. I just dropped my head. I didn't want him to see the look in my eyes – yet. There'd be plenty of time for that once we got in the ring.

I followed Uncle Pete and the club manager across the room to the gloves table behind the ring area in a relatively quiet corner of the club. Pete almost immediately started putting the huge gloves on me. Alongside me, my opponent Adam and two of his mates turned up and started doing likewise. They did up his gloves quicker than me, which seemed to suggest he'd been in the ring a few times before. He and his mates then strolled back to their table.

Pete was just tying the second knot on my gloves when the club manager asked, 'You ready, lads? '

I nodded, 'Yeah.'

Across at his table, my opponent Adam did the same thing.

At that moment my dad stood up at his table and also shouted, 'Yeah' at the top of his voice. I felt a bit embarrassed. Then the old man turned to me and said. 'Watch his hands. They're fast. Get in there and do it, Son.' I wasn't really sure if I wanted his advice or not but I didn't have any choice. I grimaced. My old man was irritating me. I'd made myself very nervous although I was glad I hadn't got the old boy with the beer gut who'd won the contest before me. My breathing suddenly got much heavier. I could feel my heart thumping away. I was no longer aware of anything other than myself. I was locking myself off emotionally, just the way I'd been taught when I was a proper boxer.

I was stood next to the ring and started doing some warm-up shadow boxing in a mirror, twisting my neck, generally loosening up. My opponent was still sitting chatting with his mates at the table across the other side of the ring. Why wasn't he getting up? Perhaps he was so confident he didn't have to bother warming up?

Suddenly I heard one of his mates shouting across the room. 'He's a bit flash, ain't he?'

Another quipped at my direction, 'Thinks he's a bit tasty, does he?'

Just then my old man shot up from his table. 'Shut yer mouth, you fuckin' prat.'

I glanced across at my dad. I knew he meant well, but the last thing I wanted was a pub brawl before I'd had a chance to show off my skills in the ring. I looked daggers at the old man and he seemed to get the message and sat down.

Meanwhile the club manager was leaning over the ropes taking late bets from the crowd. I noticed there was a lot more interest in this bout. Did they all know something I didn't?

My opponent Adam was still at his table. It seemed to be part of his act to be casual about the whole thing. Was it all a trick? His mate was even feeding him a pint through a straw because he couldn't hold the glass on account of his gloves being on. His mates then laughed snidely over in my direction. I could hear them dissing me but I ignored it all. I carried on shadow boxing in front of the mirror. My image was multiplied by six thanks to other mirrors nearby.

Then I stopped the warm-up. I shook my wrists and arms and finally looked up and focused in on my opponent Adam. I caught him looking up at me and gave him a cold, hard stare. It was the first time I'd stared him properly in the eye. Adam looked right back at me. But his eyes seemed glazed and the pupils were beady and dark as treacle. Maybe he was on drugs or something? Or maybe he was just that sort of person.

Seconds later he finally got up and walked to the ringside. He did a bit of what I'd call token shadow boxing as he walked around the tables towards me and the club manager standing by the edge of the ring.

'Ready, lads?' asked the club manager.

'Yeah.'

Adam leaped over the ropes and into the ring in one fluid movement that seemed to suggest he was good on his feet, despite all the boozing.

I didn't immediately follow him because Uncle Pete was whispering instructions right in my lug hole.

'You alright?'

'Yeah, yeah. I'm up for it. No problem.'

At that moment the club manager put his foot on the bottom rope and lifted the middle up. I got in the ring slowly. Make your opponent relax, was what I'd always been taught.

I headed straight to the middle where the ref and my opponent Adam were waiting.

'Keep it clean, lads,' said the club manager. But his words melted into the crowd by this stage. I'd only got one thing on my mind.

As we both tapped gloves reluctantly, I saw Adam look across at his mates. I couldn't hear what they were mouthing but they obviously thought he was going to cruise it. The noise was deafening. Then I heard Uncle Pete and my dad shouting at me:

'Go on, Son.'

'You'll have him.'

They both clutched pint mugs in their hands:

Me and Adam went back to our respective corners. Then the ref dropped his hand and we were off. I deliberately walked slowly out towards Adam. I wanted him to come to me. His hands were down by his side. He was either brilliant or untrained. I had a feeling he didn't know what he was doing. I thought he'd take a run at me there and then, just like the previous fighter had done in his contest.

But instead he started goading me and beckoning me towards him. I held back. I wasn't going to let this arsehole control the contest. Pete and my old man had other ideas.

'Get in there, Son,' Uncle Pete screamed above the crowd.

'Come on. Get on with it;' the crowd screamed, baying for blood.

'Give him a hiding, Son.'

Then Adam finally took two steps in my direction. That was enough for me. That was the signal. I immediately hit him with my long-reach jab to see how he'd respond. It worked a treat because he then took a wild swing at me with both fists and completely missed, smacked nothing more than the hot, smoky air.

Soon I'd got into my stride with my favourite Ali shuffle routine, the one that used to get them really pissed off back at the gym in East London. As Adam grew more and more frustrated and kept trying to swipe me with wild, inaccurate punches, I got down low, under his arms. I threw a strong right then a left into his ribs. I heard him groaning as that punch connected. The crowd was at top volume by now. I couldn't hear a thing from Pete or my dad.

Then I stepped back to see what kind of damage I'd inflicted. This time his guard was up high and he was covering himself up, looking like a frightened deer. He was shocked and stunned. Blood was coming from his lip and a cut above his eyebrow. I'd also clearly winded him because he couldn't stand up straight. He made no attempt to come back at me so I went in really hard. I was buzzin' for it by now. I could smell victory out of his fear.

Then he surprised me by managing to land a few straight punches to my forehead as I charged in. It stopped me for a few seconds before I got him with one of my finest left hooks. It was a short, sharp blockbuster and he visibly wobbled. But then he came back with a couple of defensive punches so I went in with short right jabs followed by another left hook to the side of his head.

He veered across me and then paused for a moment. I thought he was winded. Then his eyes rolled and he lurched across the rope and vomited right onto the table where all his piss-taking mates were sitting. They shot up like a bunch of schoolgirls to try and avoid the spew, but two of them caught it full on. I stood watching it in disbelief – it was bloody brilliant.

Then the ref jumped into the ring. But I hadn't finished yet. As Adam turned around, I aimed another flurry at him. I was just about to land a bone-cracking left when the ref and Uncle Pete pulled me off him. For a few seconds I kept punching out, as if I was on autopilot. Then I blinked and noticed for the first time what an awful state my opponent was in, and stopped immediately.

It was only then I realised the crowd was going wild for me. That gave me the best buzz I'd ever felt in my life. It was wicked – like a shot of adrenaline in the arm. Then I noticed the look of pride on the faces of Uncle Pete and my dad. They both looked chuffed to bits. A couple of feet away, Adam was carried out of the ring by his spew-covered mates. They didn't even dare give me a second glance.

I acknowledged the crowd with a huge wave and a little bit of shadow boxing. They loved it. I got out of the ring and went with Uncle Pete to the glove table.

'Well done, Son,' said the old man. 'What an operator. Fuckin' brilliant!'

'You done it, Boy,' said Uncle Pete as he took off the gloves. 'You fuckin' done it.'

'That's a vicious left hook you got, Son,' said the old man, so pissed he was mumbling his words. I felt like saying he would have known all about my punches if he'd bothered to watch me boxing when I was a kid.

Dad stood there, pint in hand, laughing and patting me on the back like we were the closest father and son in the world. But all I kept thinking was why the fuck wasn't he there alt those years earlier when I'd really needed him? It didn't make me happy that he was proud of me, because he didn't deserve my love that day. I didn't say a word to him. But I caught his attention with a hard, cold look straight into his face. I wanted him to know that all was far from perfect between us.

Nevertheless, all of us had some celebrating to do that evening. We got back to our table and I had a pint or two – I needed something to water down the adrenaline rush. I felt as tense as a board. I shook from the excitement for hours afterwards. My opponent, Adam, returned to his table eventually, having cleaned up. I walked over to him.

'You alright?' I asked.

'I'll live,' he mumbled back through a swollen lip.

We then both shook hands.

'You here next week?' I asked.

He laughed. 'Yeah. But I'm not goin' back in there!' he said, nodding towards the ring.

This time round his mates didn't take the piss. They were alright, as it turned out. We even bought each other a few bevvies that night. All's fair in love and war as they say.

Then, to top it all, the brunette stripper who'd caught my eye earlier came over to our table, lent across my uncle Pete, planted a lovely wet kiss on my bruised lips and said: 'You gonna buy me a drink, then?'

My uncle and the old man were giggling like a couple of schoolboys. She was wearing nothing but skimpy black lacy underwear and a pair of strappy shoes. She said her name was Susan and, naturally, I was convinced she had a twinkle in her eye for me. I bought her a rum and blackcurrant and we talked for a couple of minutes before she had to go back on stage.

Then I was handed £35 for that first fight by the club manager. Me, my uncle and the old man went off for a slap-up meal. It was the least we all deserved.

Afterwards I went to Scamps – as a paying customer for a change. That £35 had burned a hole in my pocket and I was out to enjoy every penny of it. Within minutes of walking into Scamps I bumped straight into Susan, the stripper I'd met earlier at Lacey Lady's. She looked even better off-duty: blue eyes, lovely long-flowing brown hair, about five-feet-seven. She said she was nineteen. Of course I never told her I was just sixteen. Naturally, I got her another rum and black for good measure.

At Scamps that night the doormen were all talking about my prize-fight victory. That one small dust-up helped earn me a bucket load mare respect. I was standing up straight, chest out proudly as they all came up and slapped me on the back. I was turning into a bit of a minor celebrity.

Even Dave, the manager at Scamps, had heard about my exploits. As I stood there with this tasty bird on one arm and lots of people calling me a hero, I decided that maybe the prize-fight game was worth having a proper go at. Uncle Pete had said the money would quickly get a lot better and, in any case, I loved the buzz of it all.

Aged just sixteen, I was a doorman with a reputation as a decent scrapper. People looked up to me for the first time in my life. Even the old man began treating me with more respect. Our positions were reversing. Now he wanted to keep me happy, but he knew I was still far from happy with him: All the staff at Scamps were telling him what a brilliant geezer I was. I understood why he felt so proud, but he needed to do more for me before I could forgive him for everything that had happened in the past.

That night at Scamps they were. a bit short of doormen at the end of the evening so I helped out when it came to escorting the manager Dave with all the takings over to the bank deposit machine across the street. We also had to accompany him to his house, in case there were any robbers lurking in the bushes.

I didn't mind helping out. The doormen and staff at Scamps had already become like my new family. I felt safe and secure in their company and I didn't want to do anything to risk losing them. For the first time in my life I had a purpose, a goal to fulfil. But how long would it last?

## CHAPTER EIGHT

# The Full Distance

Soon after that first fight, my old man once again drifted out of my life. He was up to his usual tricks, ducking and diving, and I soon heard on the grapevine he'd hotfooted it to Cyprus. So Uncle Pete became even more of a father figure. Sometimes I wondered how two brothers could be so different. Pete had always looked after my dad and now he was looking after me.

I had four more prize fights in quick succession at clubs near where I was living with Uncle Pete in Croydon. One opponent head-butted me as we tapped gloves to start the fight. He was like a madman on amphetamines but luckily he didn't manage a full head butt so I quickly recovered and gave him a thrashing.

The second fight went the full distance but I was never in any real danger. My opponent was like a human punch-bag, soaking up punishment and walking right back at me for more and more punches. I won on the verdict from the ref. Afterwards, when I bought my opponent a couple of beers, I realised he was so brainless he just didn't feel pain like other normal human beings.

But it was in the dark depths of Brixton that I came closest to a few problems. I was fighting in the back of a notorious boozer called The Crooked Billet, taking on a local boy who made George Foreman look like Twiggy. I eventually knocked this big bruiser out with a hammer left but the crowd were far from happy on account of the fact I wasn't a local, so me and Uncle Pete made a run for it before the crowd could rip us to shreds. We were just pushing our way out of the boozer through a sea of nasty, unfriendly faces, when an older fellow called Bill came up and introduced himself to us. He complemented me on my fighting skills and blagged a ride with us in Uncle Pete's motor. I'll never know to this day if he and Pete had planned that meeting all along but at the time I thought he seemed a decent enough fellow.

Bill was silver-haired with a broken boxer's nose. He was about 5ft 6in tall, tubby but not fat, and immaculately dressed in a single-breasted Krays-style black suit with brogues and a yellow tie. He must have been in his late fifties. He barked out in an East End cockney twang while sucking on a fat cigar; which annoyed me because I hated the smell. He made lots of hand movements as he spoke, and he boasted that his wallet was always filled with cash. I was intrigued by the big signet ring on his left hand and a watch that must have been worth a couple of grand.

Me, Bill, Uncle Pete and another of Pete's doorman mates stopped for a pint once we'd got out off the manor that night in Brixton. Bill and Pete seemed to have a lot to talk about so I played a few rounds of pool with the other doorman. Every now and again, I'd look up from the game and spot both of them looking in my direction. I got the distinct feeling they were talking about me but I was too shy, and young, to go over and ask them what it was all about.

Eventually we left the boozer and dropped Bill off at a cab rank in Streatham. That night, back at Uncle Pete's place, he told me that Bill had asked him if I'd be interested in earning 'a lot more money' in a 'different class' of fighting. Pete made it clear that he wasn't over keen on it as he felt he was responsible for me. 'It's heavy stuff. It's full monty bare-knuckle and it can end up costin' you more than just a few bruises.'

I took Pete's advice on board. Bare-knuckle wasn't really what I was after and I'd heard some horror stories about the injuries inflicted during bouts. What I really wanted was to go back to proper boxing or stick to the prize fighting with the big gloves. It seemed more respectable. But all I'd earned up to then was a maximum of £100 a fight. No more was said about the subject that night and I went to bed without really giving it a second thought.

A couple of weeks later I decided it was time to head back to East London and stay with my mum. Terry had finally abandoned the manor so the coast was now clear. I'd missed mum a lot and I knew she'd been worried about me while I'd been away in Croydon. I'd enjoyed it in South London but I wanted to get home and pick up where I'd left off. I didn't want to run away from my responsibilities. I didn't know what sort of job I'd do, but was fed up of my mum asking when I was going to come home!

\* \* \*

It soon felt good to be back amongst my old mates in Forest Gate. I quickly got myself fixed up working two days a week as a hod-carrier for a bricklayer. Some mornings I also did the bottling up at a pub where my mum worked, which meant stacking the shelves. And most weekends I was out pubbing and clubbing.

One Sunday afternoon me and two of my mates called Jimmy and Terry – both very skilful ex-amateur boxers – went down the Prince of Wales boozer, in High Street, Seven Kings, near Forest Gate. They reckoned there was a prize-fighting contest every weekend and I couldn't resist having a look at the standard of fighters on display. The Prince of Wales was a massive pub/club similar to some of the places back in Croydon but on a bigger scale. I'd been very careful not to tell a soul about what I'd been up to in South London. Not even my mum knew. Uncle Pete had said that was the best way to keep things.

That first Sunday I went down to the Prince of Wales, they had a residential champ from the previous week who'd taken on all comers and won every contest. The locals rated him as a tasty fighter. The moment I saw the makeshift ring, my heart jumped a few beats as I thought back to my previous prize-fighting bouts. I missed fighting and I was itching to get back in the ring, but I was there at the Prince of Wales with my mates and I didn't want them to see me in action. My older brother John also joined us and I certainly didn't want him blabbering to Mum about what I'd been up to.

I can't deny that fighting had been in the back of my mind ever since I'd got back on my manor. But I'd also started enjoying a bevvy and the company of girls, and I was still only a youngster. Also, I wasn't as fit as I'd been in Croydon, although hod-carrying did keep me in reasonable nick. I was having a right laugh with my mates for the first time in my life. I had enough money to get out and have a good time. What more could a sixteen-year-old want? I didn't say a word to anyone that day at the Prince of Wales and just watched the bouts with my fists clenched tightly, thinking about how I could so easily have gone in that ring and made mincemeat of every fighter I saw.

I stayed strong and resisted the temptation. I was trying to carve out a new life for myself. But seeing those fights did persuade me to get another job working a club door. This time I started minding at a place called Lords, in Ilford. At least being a doorman meant I could have the occasional dust-up without getting myself into trouble or disclosing my past involvement in the fight game.

At Lords, I was part of a well-established doorman firm and was paid £50 a night, which was good money in those days; thirty quid a night had been the going rate down in South London. It only took a couple of weeks before trouble flared up when Lords hosted an over-25s night. There was a fight between some Essex boys who'd turned up and some of the door firm keeping an eye on the dancefloor. Two bouncers called Bob and Ted ended up with torn jackets and bloody noses, and the club manager did a midnight runner because he thought someone was about to rob him. I ended up taking out a couple of older punters with a flurry of useful lefthanders, which helped calm it all down real quick. The cozzers turned up after this little barney was finished so we all went through the motions with them to convince them nothing serious had happened. As the suspicious cozzers finally left, one of the older doormen came up to me.

'You're a bit useful, son. You were pickin' that lot off like wooden tops.'

'Thanks,' I answered, trying to sound professional and a lot older than sixteen.

This fella then pointed out I was the only doorman not armed with a cosh. Some even had rubber bike grips packed with lead, which were called 'Co-Joes' – don't ask me why. Others had rubber mallets and one or two used something I thought was a bloody outrage: squirty lemon juice containers filled with ammonia.

'I prefer using my bare fists, a bit of fancy footwork and the occasional head butt,' I told the other doorman. And that was the way I wanted to keep it.

Not long after the fight, my firm of doormen decided we should mount a takeover bid for security at the nearby Ilford Palais. We had a five-on-five tear-up with the existing firm in the club car park. It ended up evens so the takeover never materialised, although I did manage to take out two of their blokes, which got me even more rave notices on the manor.

Around that time I started also working at private parties as word of my 'security skills' spread. Some of these functions were held in private halls while others hired me to mind the door to their giant; fuck-off mansions in places like Chingford and Loughton. I copped £50-£80 a night so it was very useful extra dough at the time.

Then I moved to working the doors at the Charleston Club, in Leytonstone High Road. It was a busy place and the work was non-stop. I was also doing daytimes on building sites as a hod-carrier. To be honest about it, I was feeling like a slave to my wages. I didn't seem to have any spare time and no personal life. Trying to date girls anywhere apart from in the club was virtually impossible.

Then, out of the blue, I got a call from Uncle Pete. He asked me to a party back down in Croydon because he was off to live in New Zealand. He'd had enough of the ratrace. I had a real soft spot for Uncle Pete. He'd been like a father to me in many ways, so the least I could do was go down to South London. All the old faces were at Pete's house for his party. Most of them still worked as doormen. It was a great night. A lot of beer was drunk and everyone got very merry.

A whole bunch of us stayed on at Uncle Pete's house that night and we all ended up playing ping-pong in his garage between pints. Pete pulled me aside at one stage and started asking me all about my life back in east London. I think he'd missed my company since I'd moved out of Croydon and he was genuinely interested in my future. Then another voice butted in. 'You still fighting ... ?'

I turned round to find myself face to face with the old bloke, Bill, who'd hitched a ride with us after that hairy contest in Brixton. I didn't hesitate to answer. 'Only when I'm workin' the door.'

'You and me should have a chat,' said Bill.

Just then Pete interrupted. 'Don't start on all that.' He seemed irritated at Bill for even talking to me.

Bill went a bit quiet after that and backed right off. But just as he was leaving Pete's house about an hour later, he slipped me his phone number. 'Might be able to earn you some extra cash,' he muttered, well out of Uncle Pete's earshot.

The next morning I drove back to East London with Bill's number burning a bit of a hole in my pocket. I kept wondering about whether I should call him. Certainly, I was anxious to find an easier way of earning money without having to work every hour of the day. After I got indoors, I took Bill's card out and pinned it up on a notice board that hung over my bed. On it were loads of cards given to me by people aver the years. I made a point of not telling a soul about Bill and how he'd given me his phone number.

That night I lay on my bed, arms behind my head, looking up at Bill's card, wondering whether I should give him a bell. I shut my eyes and thought of the fight game and immediately felt the adrenaline rush streaming through my body. The thrill. The butterflies. I was still living at home and hadn't gone out that night because I was strapped for cash. Maybe if I called up Bill I might not have to worry about money ever again ...

CHAPTER NINE

# Deadly Game

'Hello, Bill. It's Carl ...' I was about to say my last name but he interrupted with lightning speed.

'I thought you'd call.'

I took a deep breath. I was more nervous than before the start of a fight.

'Before I agree to anythin' I wanna know what I'm gettin' myself into.'

'No problem.'

We arranged a meeting for the following evening after Bill said he had something to show me south of the river. I didn't know what he was on about but I thought it was worth a spin. That evening, Bill was waiting in his five-year-old Jag at Lewisham Station. He had that yellow tie on again. He said very little as we drove straight to an industrial estate. Bill was a bad driver, very erratic. He was always braking suddenly, as if he had the weight of the world on his shoulders and just wasn't concentrating.

As his Jag approached a vast, grey warehouse, I spotted a heavy-looking fella in front of the main door. Its metal shutters then started opening automatically to let us in. Bright lights illuminated the inside of the warehouse. I immediately spotted loads of flash motors and people walking around the inside of the warehouse. The vehicles were expensive – Rollers, Mercs, Jags, you name it. I was gob-smacked. This wasn't another afternoon with the boys down at Lacey Lady's.

'This is the real thing,' muttered Bill as the Jag crept slowly along the inside wall of the huge warehouse. 'None of your prize-fightin' bare-knuckle bollocks. We're talkin' big money 'ere. Last man standirr' takes the prize.' I later found out that this sort of fighting had been going on for years but always stayed well underground. A world few people knew about, but where the stakes were high and the fighter's lives were on the line.

As we slowly rolled to a halt between two sparkling limos I realised the cars had been carefully parked in a circle creating a ring area in the middle. People were walking around with huge wads of cash in their hands.

After Bill carefully parked up, we got out of the Jag and I followed behind him as he stopped and greeted at least half a dozen heavy-looking geezers in overcoats. When he got to the last fella, I saw him take a fat envelope out of his inside jacket pocket. Looked like it had thousands in it.

'All of it on Gary,' Bill said to the other fells, obviously a bookie. But there were no betting slips. The stakes were far too high for anyone to ever contemplate they might get ripped off. As Bill had already said, this was the big time.

Then we strolled back to his car, got in and waited for the action to begin. I noticed that all the people – mainly well-dressed blokes – had an attitude to them. They held themselves in a certain way. Their shoulders rolled as they walked. Many of them talked out of the side of their mouths and they had tons of gold jewellery.

The floor of the warehouse was concrete and I wondered to myself if it caused a lot of extra injuries to anyone falling hard on it. The building itself had a glass ceiling and masses of lights hanging from it. Back time the doors opened and shut, the noise echoed through the entire warehouse. It was a spooky set-up. I certainly didn't feel safe in there.

Then Bill turned to me: 'Reckon you could handle it?'

'Depends how much?' I said, nibbling unashamedly at the bait.

'Thousands, son. Fuckin' thousands.'

Just then the vast warehouse doors rolled up yet again and a black BMW with blacked-out windows cruised in. Bill's eyes snapped across at the pimp-mobile. Seconds later another vehicle sped in.

The Beemer pulled up on the edge of the group of cars and I could just make out four men. Three of them got out snappily. They looked like armed heavies with their sunglasses and bullnecks. They were casting around, casing the joint. Just then the fourth man emerged. He was more bulky, dressed in jeans and a tight T-shirt. He wore heavy Chelsea-style boots and wasn't wearing any gloves. But I knew immediately that he must be one of the fighters.

On the opposite side of the main group of parked cars, a similar scene occurred moments later with the fellas in a Merc. All the cars encircling the ring had their dipped headlights on to help illuminate the fight area. Both fighters then started walking through a gap between the vehicles towards opposite sides of the ring. It was like a Hollywood movie. Surreal is the only way to describe it: fucking surreal.

Each trainer walked in front of his man, with two minders immediately to the front and back of the fighter. I could barely make out either of the fighters' features except that they both seemed to be dark and swarthy. I learned later that this was quite deliberate so that no-one got a good enough look at the fighters to point the finger at them in a court of law.

The 'ringmaster' – that's what Bill called him – was already in the space between the cars, awaiting the fighters. 'You watchin' this?' asked Bill in an almost impatient voice, without moving a muscle in my direction. I nodded. I was transfixed, glued to my seat, so to speak. It was clear that Bill didn't want us to leave his motor. Virtually everyone else remained in their limos because, as Bill later told me, 'They're not the sorta faces who want to be spotted out in the open.'

However, there were a few women out there, dripping with jewellery and fur coats. They sort of added to the atmosphere. A lot of them looked like brasses, but some of them might have been genuine wives – old-fashioned crims are surprisingly good at keeping their marriages intact.

My window was open throughout and I could hear bets being laid left, right and centre. The bookies stood out like sore thumbs. They even had the same kind of suitcases with legs underneath that they use at racetracks up and down the country. Every time a suitcase opened, I spotted the banknotes spilling out.

Just then the ringmaster took centre stage. There was a hush in the audience. 'The fight is about to commence,' he yelled in the echoing warehouse. 'All bets must be in now.'

Meanwhile each fighter was shadow boxing behind two minders on the edge of the ring. But the sheer size of the minders still meant it was virtually impossible to see the fighters clearly.

The ringmaster then slowly backed his way out of the ring. The minders separated and the fighters began walking to the centre. They moved slowly and stood upright and fearless. Bill's Jag was one of the motors parked right at the front so we had one of the best views in the warehouse.

Seconds later they were both in the ring, prowling the perimeter like caged animals. The ringmaster raised both his arms at the same time. That was the signal. The ringmaster ducked between two Rollers and the fight commenced.

No time for formalities. They were off with a vengeance. Headbutts, kicking, biting. I was astounded. The aim was victory by any means. My jaw dropped to the floor as I watched these two men brutalise each other. The ferocity of the fight was breathtaking. I could feel tension in my own stomach just watching them grinding each other down with the type of sheer unadulterated violence I'd never witnessed before in my entire life.

They bounced off at least half a dozen of the nearest cars. At one stage, one of them appeared to drop to the floor unconscious, only to be grabbed back up by the hair by his opponent, who then rammed his head against the grille of a brand new Mercedes 500 SL. Then he collapsed to the floor, out cold. The other bloke continued kicking him as he lay on the concrete. He seemed to be trying to kill him.

This put all those prize fights in the shade. This was brutal, terrifying and, I hate to say it, awe-inspiring.

The entire bout only lasted about a minute and a half. The victor signalled his win by stopping in his tracks and spitting onto the floor next to his opponent, who was out cold or maybe even dead. Then the victor turned and walked out of the ring, his minders closing in on him as he strutted towards his Beemer between all those other flash motors. The doors of both fighters' cars had remained opened throughout the fight, to make sure they could make a fast getaway in case of trouble. Already, some of the well-dressed audience were spitting and cursing in the direction of the loser. They'd no doubt lost a packet by betting on him.

As the winner headed back to his vehicle, a cacophony of car hooters started blasting away, showing their approval. Others put their headlights on full beam, showering the warehouse with fingers of sharp, white light.

Then I looked back in the ring to see the loser being dragged towards the same Merc that had brought him in just a few minutes earlier. Then, a screech of tyres as the winner disappeared through the electronically controlled doors. Back in the warehouse, the loser's minders were desperately trying to revive him with a towel before shoving him in the back of the Merc. Eventually they picked him up off the floor and bundled his crumpled body in the back seat before speeding off. Some people were still screaming abuse as the motor careered out of the building.

'Fuckin' wanker,' said one brassy-looking blonde, who I wouldn't want to get on the wrong side of.

'Useless prat,' screamed an old boy with a long overcoat and badly fitting wig.

Just then Bill chipped in, 'What d'you reckon, then?'

I was still gobsmacked by the whole event.

'Fuckin' amazin'. I'm definitely on for it.'

'Good,' said Bill, as he flicked his electronically controlled window down and a hand passed in an even fatter envelope than the one he'd handed over a few minutes earlier.

As his window buzzed back, Bill fired up the Jag along with just about everyone else in that warehouse. The noise of all the engines starting up at virtually the same time was eerie and deafening. Then the fumes started wafting through the Jag, combining with the steam from the cold. It left the entire warehouse filled with drifting smoke.

'You have to get out quick,' explained Bill. 'Specially the ones who've just lost a packet.' I just nodded. What more could I say?

Bill drove me back across the water and took me all the way to Stratford tube station that night. I made him drop me well away from home as I didn't want him knowing anything about my life. I had a feeling he was someone who'd shoot me if it suited him. As I got out, he leaned over and tapped my arm. 'It's up to you, son.'

I nodded. I didn't believe it was up to me. He was in charge of my destiny and I knew he'd be making a lot more dough than me if I turned out to be a winner. I was just about to shut the door when he pulled a handful of clean, crisp banknotes out of his pocket.

'I don't need it,' I said firmly, still wanting time to consider my decision.

'It's a day's wages for being there today.'

I shut my eyes for a moment. But his hand was still there when I opened them again.

'Alright,' I said, taking the notes and wondering if I'd live to regret my decision.

'Gissa bell when you're ready.'

He knew he had me in the bag.

I walked two miles home that night. It was a long, thoughtful stroll through my life in a sense. What did I want out of life? Was it money? Or was it revenge for all the shit that had been thrown at me for so long? Whatever the answer, I knew that Bill was standing over me like the grim reaper waiting for me to confirm my contract with the devil.

Shall I or shan't I? What happens if I lose? Would I even live to tell the tale? And even if I did live, would I be a cabbage after suffering one beating too many?

With all this swimming through my mind I stopped at my local – the Camden Arms – for a pint. At the bar I bumped into a mate called Scott.

'You look like you've seen a ghost,' he said. 'What's wrong, mate?'

I put a brave face on things, 'I've just seen somethin' so fucking unreal you wouldn't believe it if I told you.'

'What you on about?'

'Nothin'. Just buy me a pint and shut up.'

I was stunned by what I'd just witnessed. That night the booze went straight to my head and I was virtually legless by my third pint. I hadn't eaten all day and Scott ended up carrying me home to my mum's.

Next morning I felt so weird about what I'd witnessed at that fight that I retched up in the bathroom. The trouble was I could so easily see myself as one of those very same fighters. I had the right background, the right experience and probably the right attitude. You see, at that time I hated most of the fucking world. I didn't owe anyone outside my family anything. I wanted to be somebody. Somebody who earned respect within my community. Someone people would look up to. Maybe even somebody to be feared.

And then there was the money. It would be handy. More than handy. It could give me a lift up into another sphere. Then I tried to slap some sense into myself. How could I even be seriously considering it? This fight game was sick and twisted – and a highly dangerous contest. One that should be avoided at all costs.

For the next couple of months I thought a lot about Bill and the illegal fight scene. At first I kept my training up, although I still insisted to myself I'd never actually phone Bill and ask to be counted in. Trouble was that on the work front things were not looking good. The building game had virtu-ally dried up and I couldn't get many door jobs at clubs. I was scraping the barrel and my mum was barely able to afford to run our little home, let alone support her grown-up son. Soon my training started to fade as well.

I didn't have the dough to buy myself any decent clobber or even buy a girl a rum and blackcurrant at my local boozer. I kept wondering about that pot of gold awaiting me if I picked up the phone and dialled Bill's number. His card was still hanging over my bed at home, tempting me every night.

CHAPTER TEN

# **The Love of My Life**

I first met Carole in 1983 when I was working the door in the Charleston Club in Leyton. I'd run into quite a few girls through working in clubs, but I noticed her because she was the only one in a crowd wearing a tracksuit. When she appeared at the door, I told her she was too young to come in, which as it turned out was a bit strong of me as I later found out she was three months older than me (we were both seventeen). She glared at me in a fearless kind of way and I immediately clocked there was something about her that I really liked, so I waved her in with her mates.

Later that night I was on roaming duty at the club, which meant I had to wander around the premises and make sure no trouble flared up. I was near the bar when I noticed Carole and her mates again. I offered to buy her a drink on the QT but she refused. I shrugged my shoulders, smiled at her for a few moments and then walked away. It just wasn't my style to be a pushy bloke. I've always had too much respect for women to do that. After all, where would we men be without them?

That night I was back on duty at the door when Carole was leaving. I don't know what came over me. but I asked her for her phone number. I was expecting a right mouthful for being so upfront. Instead she said, 'Alright' and wrote it down. I was well chuffed. My brother, who was drinking in the club that night, even had a go at me because he thought Carole looked too young to date. But I knew there was something about her I really liked.

So I went home a happy man that evening, determined to ring her and ask her out. Next morning I spent at least half an hour plucking up the courage before I finally dialled her number. It turned out to be a wrong number. I tried it again over and over just in case. Then I moved some of the digits round but it was a complete dud. I screwed up the piece of paper and threw it in the bin. I was heartbroken. She'd obviously not felt the same way about me.

A few weeks later I was off duty, having a bevy at the Charleston when in walks Carole – bold as brass. Naturally, I completely blanked her, convinced she wanted nothing to do with me. Then she came up to me.

'D'you remember me?'

'Yeah, you did me up like a kipper.'

'Well, here's your chance to buy me a drink.'

And off we went. We went out at least three times that first week. She was the best thing that ever happened to me – and she still is to this day.

Carole was such a special creature to me. She didn't fall into all the usual categories and she wasn't a noisy Essex girl. She was a straight-talking, polite but strong-willed teenager. And she really wanted to be in my company because of who I was, not because I could get her into a club free or because she thought I was the local hardman.

She was quiet, but when she spoke her mind she meant it. She never shouted. I liked the fact that she always wore casual clothes like jeans and trainers. There were no airs and graces to Carole. What you saw was what you got. And I knew she was someone I could trust, which was probably the most important thing in my life at that time.

Carole was into volleyball big time and I used to watch her play once a week and then use the gym facilities for free. Something in the back of my mind kept telling me to keep my fitness up – just in case.

I spent most of my time at Carole's house because it was cheaper than going out. And my car was a right joke – a rusting white ex-police Triumph 2000. You could still see where the police stickers had been ripped off it. And there were holes in the dash where the two-way radios and other equipment had been.

Carole, bless her, didn't care about stuff like that. But I gotta admit it really got to me. So one night I picked up the phone and dialled Bill's number. This was it; decision time.

'Let's meet up,' he said without a hint of surprise at my call. He knew he'd already reeled me in the last time we'd met.

A few days later we met up in what was then the West Ham and England soccer star Bobby Moore's pub, called Mooro's, in Stratford. I still didn't want Bill knowing where I lived because if my mum got any inkling of what I was up to she'd have hit the roof.

It was early evening and I got to Mooro's first. I always get to places early when I'm a bit nervous. I was sitting quietly in the corner supping a pint when Bill walked in with a mate. They both stuck out like nuns in a strip joint in their smart, neatly cut whistle-and-flutes and ties. We nodded at each other. Bill got some drinks in and then he introduced his friend. 'Grant has earned a packet out of the fight game. He doesn't look too bad on it, does he?'

What was I supposed to say? 'He does. He's a right ugly bastard.' So I just nodded politely.

'Right,' said Bill. 'There's a job on the go. You been doing any training?'

'Nope.'

'Well you'd better get your arse into gear, sunshine.'

Bill then asked me if I wanted to train with Grant. I replied 'No thanks. Prefer trainin' on my own.' I didn't know who the fuck Grant was so I wasn't keen on turning him into my new best friend.

Five minutes later – after a bit of small talk and banter – Bill and I shook hands and he got up to leave with Grant.

'You need some readies?' Bill asked me, almost as an after-thought.

'Nah. I'm alright.' In my naivety I thought that if I didn't take any money off him that day then it'd be easier to back out if I wanted to.

'Gissa bell in exactly one week and I'll tell you all the details.' Then he was gone.

Fuck it, I thought to myself. Am I really going to do this? I'd shaken his hand on it and I'd been brought up to believe that a handshake was as good as a written contract. There was no way I could back out now. I was up to my ears in it. But what the hell ...

That week I went back to hod-carrying at a building site in Tottenham, North London, and tried to get down to the gym to do some running whenever I had the chance. At first, I was shocked at how unfit I'd become. A lot of it was down to the fact I'd been spending much of my time with Carole at home, instead of going to the gym.

Finding out I was so unfit made me realise that if I was serious about the illegal fight game then I needed to get properly fit again. So I didn't ring Bill a week later as he'd instructed. Instead I went through a rigorous training regime because I knew I'd be like a lamb to the slaughter if I entered a ring before I was fighting fit.

Three weeks after I was supposed to have called him, I finally picked up the phone.

'Why d'you take so fuckin' long comin' back to me?' Bill responded in a dry tone.

'Got caught up at work,' I lied.

'How's the trainin' goin'?'

I assured Bill I'd been hard at it. Then he said he'd come down and see me later that night. Obviously he was a bit twitchy about whether I really was fit again and wanted to inspect his 'goods' to make sure they were in good working order.

Three hours later I was banging away on a punchbag when Bill strolled in to the local youth hall called Maryland Point, in Stratford.

'Is there a quiet corner we can have a chat?' he asked me within seconds of arriving.

'Yeah. Just gotta shower up first.'

Ten minutes later Bill was driving me in his XJ6 to a local snooker hall called the Golden Eagle. He kept well off the subject of the fight game in the car, and conversation wasn't easy between us, especially since his driving continued to greatly trouble me. Stirling Moss he was not. There were lots of uncomfortable silences.

Once we finally got to the Golden Eagle, I got Dave the manager to put the light on table number six because it was in a corner well away from the other tables. Then I racked the balls up carefully. Bill took the break.

He smacked at them and managed to get a stripe in the far left corner pocket.

'Right, let's talk money,' he said, leaning on his cue and taking a look to see if anyone was within listening distance. Then he glanced down at what he could pot next.

'What sorta money we talkin' about?' I asked in a deadpan voice.

Bill smashed at a stripe and missed the pocket by miles.

'Works out 60/40.'

I lined up my first one of the day.

'Me 60?' I asked.

'Nah. Me 60. You 40,' said Bill.

This bloke was taking the piss. I smashed a solid brown into the middle pocket.

'But how much actual dough we talkin' about here?' I asked.

'Depends on what happens.'

I missed the next one and then looked over at him.

'What d'you mean? Who wins?'

'Yeah,' he answered as he took aim.

Bill clearly didn't like talking money because he then tried to change the conversation by suggesting I do some more work in the gym.

'Yeah I'll do it, if it makes you feel better,' I said, sounding as if I didn't give a toss.

I won the snooker game hands down. But Bill never actually specified how much money was involved and I was so desperate for a decent earner I never nailed him down properly. As I left the hall that night I wondered what the hell I was playing at.

Three days later, Bill picked me up outside Stratford bus station and had a right go at me when I slammed his precious car door too hard. That bothered me a bit, but not half as much as his rubbish driving. We eventually headed along the Whitechapel Road to Bethnal Green. Bill hardly said another word in the car after that first exchange and I didn't have a clue where we were going, except that he'd told me to bring my gym bag. Eventually he parked the Jag up in a residential street and I followed him up the steps to a big imposing Victorian house.

An old dear of about eighty let us in through the front door. I couldn't even see her face clearly because she hid behind the door as she opened it. Where the hell was he taking me? I followed Bill down a narrow hallway and through a back door into the garden. I was surprised how small the garden was. There was a one-storey building constructed at the end of it, which partly explained the size of the garden in comparison to the house.

When we reached the door to the building, it was swung open by a fit-looking ex-boxer type in his late forties. Inside were two heavy bags hanging from the ceiling and a small-sized ring. It was like an Aladdin's cave amongst the rose bushes.

The ex-fighter turned round and walked back to hold one of the bags for a wiry-looking fella who was slugging the hell out of it. It all looked like a bit of a show for me. Then Bill broke the ice by introducing me.

'This is the boy I was tellin' you about,' he said to the older ex-fighter, completely ignoring the bloke doing the punching.

Just then the boy on the bag stopped whacking it. The ex-fighter shook hands with him and the kid disappeared out the back. Bill nodded to a bench next to the bags and I sat down and changed into my boots and training gear. I noticed that the small ring was surrounded by ropes and even had padded corners. It was a thoroughly professional training set-up. Maybe Bill had a stable of fighters, I thought to myself.

'Just give him a gentle warm-up,' Bill said to the ex-fighter. 'Carl, take it easy on him. We're only here to see how you're shapin' up.'

Using proper gloves, we had a nice, easy sparring session as per Bill's instructions. I jabbed away at my new partner and he lashed out a few times to see how I handled the punches. After about two minutes Bill called a halt to proceedings.

I went and sat back on the wooden bench on the edge of the ring and Bill pulled up a chair and sat down opposite me. He went through all the details of each of my early prize fights down in South London and for the first time I realised he'd been watching me at every bout. He had a dossier on me in his mind. I was impressed.

Then he got serious. 'There'll be a lot more kickin' and dirty tricks. Things you've been told not to do in the past. Now you've gotta do them, otherwise you've had it.'

I nodded keenly.

'Jimmy,' said Bill to the ex-fighter. 'Show the kid how it's done.

Jimmy then got back into the ring and started a short demonstration. First he showed me a throat punch. It's exactly that: a punch directly on the Adam's apple that knocks out a man if properly detonated. I mumbled something like 'I do know a bit about the street' to try and let them know that I was knowledgeable about such moves, but Bill and his mate took no notice. Next came close quarters kicking. Bill could see from the look on my face that I was far from impressed.

Then Jimmy turned towards me and punched his own chest lightly. Bill said: 'Solar plexus. Base of the rib cage.' Jimmy then showed how if you brought forward a couple of your knuckles you could make your fist into an even more deadly weapon. Looking back on it, a lot of the moves were pure martial arts, but I didn't know much about that at the time. Jimmy did each move in slow motion, making it all look a bit strange. I nodded my head each time. I didn't have the bottle to tell Bill I'd pulled just about every trick in the book since becoming a doorman.

At the end of the session, Bill nodded towards the door and off we headed through an alleyway behind the house. As he dropped me back in Strafford, Bill patted me on the back. 'Off you go, Son. And don't forget this is all between you and me. Less people know about it the better.'

I felt like saying I'd worked that one out. There was no way I wanted anyone to know what I was up to. My mum and brothers would have killed me, and Carole would probably have dropped me like a hot brick if I'd confessed what I was getting into.

I called Bill a couple of days later to ask him when I'd be fighting.

'It's all organised,' he said.

'So what about the money, then?' I asked.

Bill said the winner's fee was £4000 and loser would cop £1500.

'But you won't lose,' he added.

'Right,' I replied, not at all sure whether I shared his confidence.

Bill said the fight would be in two or three weeks' time. I didn't bother asking who my opponent was because I knew he'd never say. About a week or so later I called him up with a progress report on my training and to assure him I'd kept out of trouble and not had any mishaps that might threaten my fitness.

'Keep your nose clean, Son,' said Bill.

I couldn't get that oncoming fight out of my head. Soon I was living, eating, shitting and sleeping it. And there were so many questions I hadn't got around to asking Bill ... Had any fighters died? What happened if I was badly injured? Who'd get me to a hospital? But I bottled it all up and didn't tell a living soul.

I kept my head down and got on with my training. At one stage, I thought about calling Uncle Pete but I knew he'd have a right go at me. After all, I think he'd wanted me to steer clear of Bill. But all this secrecy was making me feel incredibly lonely and a bit desperate. My stomach was twisted up in knots.

And Dad had long since disappeared off the scene. I hadn't seen him since I'd been in South London. I heard from Uncle Pete that he'd moved in with yet another bird. Typical, he was never there when it really mattered. I so needed to talk to someone about the biggest dilemma I'd ever faced in my life. Then I thought about the money and the excitement of winning. And I convinced myself it would all be worthwhile in the end.

The day I had to call Bill about the date of my first fight finally arrived, and I was so nervous I couldn't eat anything or even think straight. I kept playing the words I would say over and over in my mind. Of course, when it came to the actual call it was easy as one, two, three. And Bill made it all sound so normal.

'It's on for tomorrow. Make sure you wear jeans and get yourself a pair of boots but no steel toecaps. Alright?'

'What sort of shirt do I wear?'

'A tight-fitting T-shirt or nothin' on top if you want to show off yer tan.'

No way, I thought to myself, I'll get a T-shirt. I'm not one for showing off my physique. I'm not just a piece of meat on display. I'm a proper fighter, aren't I?

Bill told me to be outside Strafford bus station. 'A car'll meet you. It'll be Jimmy, the geezer you met in the gym the other day.'

'I'll be there.'

Jimmy and a mate of his were waiting in a dark blue Volvo when I got off the bus. He waved me into the back of the car and off we went. The driver never even turned his head towards me.

'We're meetin' Bill in an hour near the location,' said jimmy.

That was it. He didn' t say another word, and although I was desperate to fire a few questions at him I knew that wasn' t the done thing. As we headed west along the Embankment I sat back and listened to Barry White playing on the stereo cassette and glanced over at the sparkling lights of Tower Bridge. Here I was with a couple of East End hardmen on my way to a prize fight that might end in my death and I didn' t even have a fucking clue where we were heading.

Eventually we got through West London and stopped at the first service station on the M4 just before Heathrow Airport. 'You want anything, Son?' asked Jimmy. The driver remained up front without moving a muscle. All I could see were the pockmarks on the back of his ugly bulldog neck.

'Nah,' I responded.

A few minutes later we were back on the M4 and Barry White was moaning and groaning away again, 'You're The First, The Last, My Everything'. We took a turn-off for Reading about thirty minutes later. A couple of miles down the road I spotted Bill's Jag slung up in a lay-by. He was in the driver's seat and there were a couple of minder types keeping him company.

As we pulled up in the lay-by, Bill got out of his Jag at the same time as his minders. They left all their doors open as if they were planning a quick escape.

I stepped out of the Volvo.

'Allright, Son? You ready for action?'

I nodded and muttered, 'Right as rain.'

Bill pointed towards the back of the jag so I got in with one of the minders. Bill and the other fella sat up front.

'It's about ten minutes away. You eaten?'

"Bout four hours back.'

'Good.'

The minders didn't utter a word. They were wearing black suits with white shirts and black ties.

'The opposition's not up to much. Bit of a fat bastard,' said Bill, as if he was talking about the weather.

'Where we fightin'?' I asked nervously, more to make conversation than because I cared. It was already too late to back out.

'Don't worry, Son. You'll be well impressed.'

I presumed by that he meant a few cars parked round in a circle like that bout he'd taken me to see in Lewisham.

A few minutes later we got to a big industrial park. It was pitch dark and most of the warehouses seemed to have closed down for the day.

The Jag then turned sharply onto a ramp up towards the front of one warehouse and in through an open double doorway. Wooden pallets lined the walls inside the building, but there was no sign of any ring or cars.

Then the car did a sharp turn to the left where a bloke was standing by a shutter doorway that was automatically opening up. Bill nodded at the fella and the Jag headed through the entrance into an alleyway between two warehouses.

'What's happenin'?' I asked Bill.

'You' ll see.'

At that moment the jag made another sharp turn off the alleyway and into the opening of the next building where another fella stood sentry at the door. This time there were lots of people and cars. Top-quality motors that were even flashier than the ones I'd seen at that fight over in Lewisham. This was it. My stomach was turning wheelies.

Then I saw something in the distance. I squinted for a moment because I couldn't quite believe it. It seemed to be built out of tubular steel and closely knitted wire mesh.

I was about to enter the cage.

CHAPTER ELEVEN

# One-Way Ticket

'Welcome to the cage,' said Bill with a slight touch of drama to his voice.

'I'm not fightin' in that.'

I felt like I'd been set up. No-one had even suggested I'd be performing in a cage. This was fucking barbaric.

'I'm not some fuckin' animal.'

'It's nothin' to worry about,' interrupted Bill calmly and without a hint of surprise in his voice. 'You stick your head through the door at the side and off you go.' But this was like something out of Roman times. Perhaps they'd chuck a couple of tigers in with us just for good measure?

But what could I do? These weren't the sort of people I'd tell to fuck off and then stroll out of that warehouse a free man. They'd tear me apart limb by limb and then feed me to the pigs. I was locked in. There was no escape. I'd have to go through with it.

As I got out of the jag, the two minders surrounded me like a protective shield. Bill walked just behind us. Just then I noticed a dark blue transit van pulling up on the opposite side of the cage. It parked up sideways on, the side door opened up and four men got out. Three of them were identically dressed in black bomber jackets. The fourth fella was my opponent. He was bare-chested, in his forties and strutting around like a bulked-up peacock. He was stocky, but had a reassuringly big belly. I smiled carefully to myself. I had the scent of a victory in my nostrils. Now I just wanted to get on with the show.

The cage itself was surrounded by a lot of men and a sprinkling of well-dressed women with coiffured hair and fur coats. Some of them looked like the faces I'd seen at that last fight in Lewisham.

The atmosphere inside the warehouse was smoky and the strong, overhead lights were shooting white beams down from the ceiling. The lamplight bounced off the metallic cage giving it a bizarre, sparkling glint. There were so many people around the cage I couldn't examine my opponent in any detail. And the noise was building.

I was so hyped up I couldn't focus on anything other than the cage itself. The crowd separated as me and my burly minders began making our way towards the cage, with Bill still just behind. The sheets of mesh metal that surrounded the cage provided me with a distorted image of the other fighter as he made a similar walk towards the cage from the opposite direction. The cage seemed to be about the same size as a normal boxing ring, only totally enclosed. The mesh roof was about nine feet high. Bill later told me that they'd invented the cage in America in the mid-'70s after crowds kept invading the ring during illegal fights. It was there to keep them out as well as trap us in it until one of us was out cold on the floor.

A voice snapped me back to reality. 'He's nothin' but a kid,' I heard one punter shout at me.

I'll show them who's the kid, I thought to myself.

Truth is, I was so nervous my gut felt like it was about to explode. My head was throbbing and my eyes were snapping around in all directions. I dipped my head down so I didn't look at everyone but then I held my head up high again as I got close to the cage. I wanted them to see there was not an ounce of fear in my eyes.

Then my minders nodded across at their opposite numbers. It was time to open the doors to the cage and I immediately noticed how small the entrance was. It couldn't have been more than three feet by three feet. One minder leaned down and snapped open the bolt. The other minder behind me then put his hand on my head and pushed me down and in through the door.

'Get in there and do him, my son,' one of them muttered at me as I hesitated for a split second. Opposite me they were going through the same routine. I crouched low in order to get through the doorway into the cage. This was it. No turning back now.

At that moment our eyes met for the first time. I've gotta have him or I'm dead, I thought to myself. No doubt he was thinking the same: As he got up inside the cage it seemed, for a moment, as if he was massive, his dark bulk silhouetted by the bright lights.

I stood up straight and turned just as he began coming straight at me like a bear on heat. He was growling. I could see the yellowing whites of his glassy eyes. His growl was getting louder. As he got closer, I stepped to my left with a nifty Ali-shuffle movement. He went straight past my right shoulder through the air. I aimed a punch at an angle right behind his ear. As I connected, he went flying into the wall of the cage, which rattled like a thousand tins of sardines.

I bounced away from him and took up a boxing stance, both feet wide apart, steady as a rock, waiting for him to come back at me again. I felt I was already in control. He tried to beckon me over. I stood my ground and ignored his battle cry so he began pacing up and down. Up and down. Up and down. It was a bit of a show for the audience. He actually thought my reluctance came from fear. He wanted me to make the same mistake he had and go after him, but I knew if I stood my ground he'd be the one in trouble.

Then it went deathly quiet around the cage. The crowd wanted action and they'd gone numb.

'Fuckin' kill him,' said one charmer, breaking the wall of silence.

'Go on, Son. Have him!' said another smooth talker.

With that last shout, my opponent snapped into action and started bounding towards me growling like a grizzly on heat again. This time he got near enough to land a flurry of punches but he only hit my upper torso, the strongest body area of all. Then he tried to pull my head down on his knee but I managed to slip out of his grasp. I punched out at him with a high-speed flurry. Right, left, right, left.

Then I put my hands on his shoulders and pulled him towards me for the perfect putting position. I aimed for the bridge of his nose and heard it crack as I connected with all the force I could muster. He stumbled backwards against the rattling cage walls once again.

Then I moved in low, stabbing uppercuts to his face and throat. He grimaced each time I connected. Soon he was blowing hard, Obviously losing his breath. A couple more uppercuts and his legs began buckling. I saw his eyes roll as he toppled backwards and slumped against the cage yet again. Then I kicked out at his lower stomach over and over again with my left foot, into his fat, blubbery gut. It was me or him out there and I couldn't afford to let him recover or else I'd end up on a slab. All or nothing.

By this time my frenzied state had completely taken over my fighting skills. I was like a madman. In some ways, I'd lost the plot. I'd never felt like this before in my entire life. I started pummelling his face as he leaned, slumped against the metal walls of the cage. Seconds later he went out like a baby on breast milk.

A white towel was thrown into the cage and the contest was over. I looked down at him on the floor for a moment and thought I saw him move so I started pummelling him just in case it was all a trick. When he didn't respond, I stopped as suddenly as I'd begun and stepped back from my victim.

Bottles were raining against the mesh wall of the cage. Little splinters of glass were crunching under my boots. I looked round and spotted Bill standing by the doorway to the cage with the two minders.

'Come on. Let's get goin'!' he yelled.

There was screaming and yelling going on all around me. I moved towards the cage door when a punter appeared alongside my minder. He'd got into the cage and was heading right for me, all fists flying. The minder took him out with one sturdy right hook. Looking back on it I reckon many of the punters were on coke or something because they were so fucking hyped up it was ridiculous. Of course, some of them were angry because they'd lost a bucketload of cash by betting on the other fighter but that didn't give them the right to have a pop at me.

I stooped down and stepped out of the cage. Then one of the minders covered me with a blanket as if I was some serial killer up at the Old Bailey. Bottles and stuff were being lobbed right at us. A few seconds later we got to the car where Bill was already revving up.

We screeched off and headed out through the two warehouses.

'Good work, Son. You've earned yourself a few bob.'

I didn't reply.

'You alright?' asked Bill, although I didn't think he really gave a fuck.

'Yeah. But me mouth is fuckin' sore.'

I dropped my gumshield out of my mouth and pulled out my cricket box. I had a split lip and two big black eyes and a handful of cuts and bruises. But it was nothing serious. As I turned to look behind us, dozens of cars were flying out of the warehouse at top speed as well.

The minders talked amongst themselves but they never said a word to me during the entire drive back to East London. It made sense since they weren't supposed to know who I was.

I allowed Bill to drive me all the way home to Forest Gate that night. I was too knackered to care if he knew where I lived. I was completely entangled.

'Call me in two days and I'll have your dough,' said Bill as we pulled up at the end of my street.

Then I turned and asked him: 'D'you think that other fella's alright?'

'Don't worry about him,' Bill snapped back.

It wasn't until a long time later that I discovered he'd died before they'd even got him to hospital.

It was almost eleven when I crept into my mum's house as quietly as possible, in the hope I could get to my bedroom without bumping into anyone. I'd made it to the bottom of the stairs when a voice called from the kitchen.

'Where you been?' yelled Mum. I stood frozen to the floor in the hallway.

'Been out for a while.'

'Come in here, darlin' and kiss your mum goodnight.'

I pulled my collar up around my face and headed sheepishly into the kitchen. But you can't fool mums that easy, can you?

'What the hell have you been up to?' she asked the moment I walked in.

'Got in a pub fight.'

'Who with?'

'Dunno.'

'What was it all about?'

I hesitated while my brain slowly clicked over as I came up with an excuse.

'Spilt my drink on some fella.'

'What? And he did that to you?'

'Bit of a hard bastard,' I mumbled.

'Come 'ere, you,' she said, putting her hand to my face to get a closer look at the wounds.

That night I let mum dab my wounds with iodine. She had a couple of girlfriends round to watch the telly and they all made a right fuss of me. She even filled a tea towel with ice and made me press it up against my face to bring out the bruising. Then she did what all good, caring mums do best and made me a cuppa. Eventually I sloped off upstairs and soaked it all off in a piping-hot bath. I was surprised at how many knocks I had, considering the short duration of the fight.

After the bath I started shaking as the realisation of what I'd just done began to sink in. I'd gone and got myself caught up in something I had little or no control over. I'd just become part of an evil world filled with dodgy fellas who considered me nothing more than a piece of meat. Then I thought about the money I stood to make. I lay on my bed looking at Bill's card once again and knew there was no turning back. This was a chance to make some big bucks that would help me settle my life once and for ever. Trouble was, I was shaking like a leaf thinking about what the future held.

So I phoned my beloved Carole to see how she was. I felt a real need to talk to her. She was asleep so I didn't manage anything more than a few mumbled words. If we'd had more of a chat maybe I would have told her and that might have been the end of it all. But I didn't and I decided to use the illegal fight game to fund both our futures.

That night I found it near impossible to sleep. I started flashing back to the fight and the dreadful state of that other fella when I left the cage. I kept seeing his bloodied, crooked face over and over again. I was obviously riddled with guilt about the state I'd left him in. I also felt bad about lying to Mum and Carole, who were two of the only people in the world I trusted. Then I thought about the sweetness of victory and how it made me feel important – as if I was somebody for the first time in my life.

The next day I ate a mountain of food and chilled out around the house. My hands and knuckles were red raw from where I'd hit the cage instead of my opponent and I didn't want to go near Carole until all the swelling had died down.

That evening I called Bill about the money. We met at midday the following day outside Stratford station. I couldn't face a drink with him so I just leant into his Jag and said I had to see someone and couldn't hang about.

'You alright?'

'Right as rain, Bill,' I replied.

He handed me the envelope. 'Here you go, Son. Don't spend it all at once.' Then he added, 'It's all there plus a bonus.' He'd whacked another £200 on top of the four grand. 'Gimme a bell in three or four weeks.'

I was still nodding unenthusiastically as his motor slipped off into the lunchtime traffic.

That first fight was still weighing heavily on my mind.

## CHAPTER TWELVE

# Green is the Colour

Truth was that the money I got from that first fight really made a big difference to my life at that time. I finally moved out of my mum's house into my own one-bedroomed flat in Atherton Road, Stratford, and I went back to hod-carrying. The cushion of the extra money plus a regular job felt very good.

About a week after moving in, I went down on one knee and asked Carole – we were both just nineteen at the time – if she'd live with me in my tiny, bare flat that contained nothing more than a bed, a fridge, a cooker and a couple of hand-me-down chairs. Oh, and I also begged her to marry me, naturally. She nodded her head so I took that as a yes and headed round to ask her dad if he'd let me be his son-in-law. He just shrugged his shoulders and said: 'Whatever Carole wants.' Carole's parents didn't like me much at first but then who could blame them?

Here I was, this big thug of a geezer who was about to steal their daughter away from them.

With a wedding on the horizon, I knew I'd have to save hard since I couldn't expect Carole's family to cough up for everything. I desperately needed the security that a marriage and children would offer. Looking back on it, I was piling pressure on myself. Carole expected a decent-sized wedding, naturally. But my money from that first fight wasn't going to cover it.

One morning I woke up and decided to call Bill and make myself available for another fight. I allowed myself to get caught up in Bill's dodgy fights again because, besides the money, I still hankered after that adrenaline rush I'd first enjoyed when I'd boxed as a kid. I wanted that feeling again – the elation, the invincibility that came with being number one. I had something to prove – to myself.

A lot of people will think I'm a nutter for even considering another fight but unless you've been in the ring you don't know how strong that bug really is. I'd been hooked since I was a kid and now I'd found something to replace boxing, which had been the love of my life. Call it a cry for attention. Call it what you like, but I was locked in.

I continued not to tell Carole what I was up to because it wasn't fair to put her through all that anguish and worry. This wasn't the best way to treat the girl I was about to marry, but you have to understand how important it was to me that -she had everything she wanted. I didn't want the problems experienced by my mum and dad and the pressures that forced them apart. Bill had also already made it crystal clear that the cage was a highly secretive world and I'd be endangering the life of anyone I spilt the beans to.

I made out to Carole that I'd started working on the door of a club in the West End, to give me the cover to begin a new, strict training regime for the next fight. Carole was working as a telephonist at BT at the time. Three evenings a week she played for the local volleyball team at the Eastway Sports Centre.

By this time I had a phone in the flat so Bill was able to call me direct. He eventually rang up and announced the next fight would be in two days' time.

'The money's good – five grand,' he said and paused. 'We're goin' over the water for this one.'

'What?' I asked.

'Just get yourself in shape. I'll do the rest,' he said, ignoring my question.

Apart from that trip to Jersey when I was a kid, I'd never been out of England. Where did he mean by across the water? It really bugged me. I didn't fancy going to a foreign place for a fight. Anything could happen abroad.

I hardly slept a wink over the next two days. I had a bad feeling in my gut about what I was letting myself in for. It wasn't helped by the fact that I couldn't talk to anyone else about how I felt.

On the day of the fight, two of Bill's heavy-looking mates picked me up in the early evening at Stratford. We headed east on the Old Southend Road. I still didn't know what 'over the water' really meant. An hour later we drove into what looked like a pitch-black field but turned out to be a small airstrip. Then I spotted Bill's Jag parked up alongside a smallish twin-engined plane. Where the hell were we going?

It was black as the ace of spades except for some small lights alongside a piece of rough tarmac that I presumed was the runway. Bill opened my door and greeted me like a longlost son, which I didn't much like. It was a performance for a bunch of fellas whose heads I could see looking our way from inside the plane. There were at least eight people already on board when I clambered in. They all seemed to know Bill and he introduced me to each of them as 'that kid I was telling you about'.

The geezers already in the plane were in their forties and fifties and they all looked as if they had a bit of form. Bill walked me to the back of the plane to meet two huge black geezers called Neville and Wayne. 'They'll look after you for this trip,' said Bill. I kept wondering why the hell I needed two huge minders: was Bill expecting some kind of aggro or what? As I nodded my head at Neville and Wayne, they winked at me in a reassuring kind of way. For some weird reason I felt safe with them. They were both wearing identical black leather bomber jackets and talked almost like twin brothers. Oh, and they were both at least six foot three and must have each weighed about eighteen stone. They were old school chums and both had strong Jamaican accents with a London twang.

Bill insisted I sat with him on the plane. It was a tight squeeze. I remember the propellers starting up very noisily, which bothered me because they coughed and spat a lot. Take-off was bumpy and the plane seemed to only just get off the ground before we ran out of crumbling tarmac. As it veered upwards, I noticed the virtually full moon backlighting the tree-tops just a few feet below us. But Bill and his cronies didn't seem to give a fig. They were passing round scotch and vodka bottles and filling themselves up as if they didn't have a care in the world.

'So where we goin'?' I asked Bill when the plane finally settled on an even keel.

'Ireland, my son,' came the response.

I wanted to ask him who my opponent was, especially since he hadn't mentioned a word about him. But I didn't have the bottle so I sat there without saying another word.

Bill totally misinterpreted my awkward silence. 'You'll get paid straight after the fight this time.'

Money was the last thing on my mind as the plane bounced up and down while we hit some turbulence. All around me the booze continued flowing. The only other people as quiet as me were the minders Neville and Wayne at the back. They both had Walkmans plugged in and were sipping out of Evian bottles. I pretended to sleep alongside Bill but my mind was buzzing with concern about the fight.

Eventually, the pilot came over the PA system. As it crackled, I wondered if he was about to tell us about engine trouble but, through his strong Irish accent, he announced our descent. He never mentioned the name of the place we were landing at but none of the old soaks on board that night cared, and they were footing the bill.

The plane coasted down so quietly I thought the pilot had switched off the engines to save petrol. We landed with a thump on a field that was littered with cowpats. Torches strapped to buckets had been turned into makeshift landing lights.

It looked like a field in the middle of nowhere. I couldn't even tell you if we were in the north or the south of Ireland but I suppose it was most probably the south. The plane sliced through a few nettles as it taxied over towards a small tin shack in a corner of the field. A white transit van and two four-wheel-drive motors were parked up. Me, Wayne and Neville plus Bill headed straight for the van. As we drove off, all I could make out were the tail-lights of the two cars in front, containing Bill's cronies. I still had a bad feeling, but there was nothing I could do about it now. I was in the middle of a strange country with a bunch of hoods about to attend a fight that might cost me my life.

I was crammed next to Neville and Wayne on a makeshift wooden bench across the back of the full-panelled transit with Bill up front with the driver. It turned out to be an even bumpier ride than on that little plane across the water. Eventually, our Irish driver spoke: 'Only about ten minutes to go, lads.'

Then we drove across a rattling cattle grid and into a farm. We were waved through by a man at the gate, who was packing a shotgun. Half a mile further down a muddy, slippery track, the van approached a big, modern corrugated-type barn sitting out in the middle of a field. The cars carrying Bill's pals drove through an opening in the barn. Just then our van stopped a hundred yards from the same entrance. Our driver pulled out a walkie-talkie, switched it on with a crackle and talked in what sounded like Gaelic.

Just then Bill – still sitting up front – turned to me and said: 'You all set, Son?'

"S'pose so,' I shrugged.

Truth was, I was far from happy. Everything about this fight didn't quite gel. Perhaps these geezers were IRA and they were planning to kill us all at the end of the fight, whatever the result? No-one would know what had happened to any of us. We were a long way from home.

'You properly warmed up?' asked Bill.

'Bit tight,' I replied.

Bill promised I'd get a couple of minutes to limber up once we got inside.

A voice came from the driver's walkie-talkie as it crackled back into life and the van moved off towards the barn. Three heavy-looking types at the door to the barn waved us in. Inside, I immediately noticed a cattle pen. The floor was muddy and smelly and the van skidded slightly. Beyond the cattle pens was a ring like a mini auditorium. We were in a cattle market. At least there was no cage this time so I wouldn't be penned in like a monkey at the zoo. But then again, I was being treated no better than cattle this time, so what was the difference?

I spotted my opponent almost immediately because he was already pacing up and down inside the ring, dressed in a big white shirt with a bright-green shamrock across his chest. The atmosphere was very different from my first fight. This time there wasn't a woman in sight and the punters looked like hard farmer types, with ruddy faces and wellies. The cars weren't so flash either, but the atmosphere was far more intimidating because this lot looked like they'd shoot you as soon as look at you.

I even spotted what looked like a few local coppers in uniforms amongst the crowd, taking their seats in the ring's auditorium. There were bales of hay everywhere and a lot of slippery cow dung.

'Who the fuck are they?' I muttered.

'Don't worry, Son,' said Bill. Then, completely ignoring my remark, he explained, 'He won't come straight at you. They have to signal first. It's part of the rules over here.'

Part of the rules? I thought to myself. Since when were there any fucking rules? But it wasn't the look of the fighter that bothered me. I was more concerned by the set-up. I couldn't see a way out of here safely if we upset any of these evil bastards.

As we jumped out of the van, Bill shook hands with an Irishman who appeared out of nowhere. The two men then led me, Wayne and Neville towards the ring area. The noise subsided a bit as we walked towards the ring. Each step seemed to throw up a handful of dust, and the lighting was curiously low, making it all seem hazy.

'You ready, Son?' asked Bill as we moved through the crowds, careful not to catch anyone's glance. I didn't reply. Ahead of me I could see my opponent screaming his head off in the ring, pacing up and down like a right nutter. I couldn't understand a word he was saying – it sounded like gibberish. But he looked much fitter than my last victim. He was in his mid-twenties, a big, tall, healthy-looking, farmer-boy type. His build was similar to mine. Just then a shiver ran through me as if someone had just walked over my grave. It was an ominous sign.

This time there was no ringmaster in sight. As we got past the cattle pens on the way to the actual ring, my eyes locked onto my opponent properly for the first time. He was trying to bore holes into my head with his gaze. I shrugged and snarled. Two could play at that game. Just then someone in the background shouted, 'Get a move on, Brit boy.'

Then another voice: 'Gonna teach you a lesson, Sonny.'

As I sauntered into the ring, Bill muttered something just before standing back: 'You're on your own now, Son.'

I was just about to say, 'What about that warm-up you

promised me?' when I turned and realised the fight had already started.

Suddenly the ring seemed to shrink in size. I looked across and my opponent was coming towards me in a boxing stance, guard up, feet apart. So I played it his way and put up my dukes. We began by punching each other like legit fighters. I liked it. Maybe this wasn't going to be a fight to the death like I'd feared after all? We were testing each other out like real boxers do at the start of a fight.

He was a fair old puncher but not that accurate, and kept catching the top of my head, which must have hurt him more than me. But he seemed to think that if he carried on punching away he'd eventually wear me out. Then I put on a bit of an Ali shuffle and soon found out he was as flat-footed as a Sumo wrestler.

I started catching him with some decent jabs. I played it very defensive, trying to wear him out. We carried on like that for what seemed like a couple of minutes. But this crowd wasn't here for a display of clean boxing. They started jeering.

My opponent reacted by coming at me with a flurry of left hooks and then a whacking right-hander. But I managed to dip low under most of his punches. Then I gave him an 'Iron Mike' fist jab in the ribs and heard them crunch, like twigs snapping. I kept stabbing away at them and heard more cracks. More body shots followed. He was soon blowing badly which meant he was in trouble. The home crowd went quiet. That silence made it easier for me to hear the damage I was inflicting on my opponent.

I finished him off with a right across the throat. He went down holding his neck and gargling. His breathing on the floor was uneven and his skin was changing colour rapidly. I stood back, waiting for him to get up.

Just then the audience came alive again. 'Cheatin' fuckin' Brit bastard.'

Maybe they'd been expecting a straight-forward bare knuckle contest, but no one had told me that before the fight. Meanwhile my opponent was still on the floor and rapidly turning purple. I looked across at Bill for some guidance. He seemed to be ignoring me. The crowd was getting more rowdy by the second.

'Arsehole Brit.'

'Teach that Brit bastard ...'

I looked across at Bill again and he shook his head. What the hell was going on? What should I do? Did I stamp on his head or stand back and risk him recovering and coming back at me?

Just then a huge fat Farmer Giles lookalike jumped into the ring from the audience. Dozens of beer bottles followed him and the crowd was stamping its feet on the floor in anger. I looked across at Neville and Wayne and they piled in to get me. Neville got caught on his cheek by a flying bottle just as we were ducking and diving our way out of the ring. What the hell was happening? I thought I'd won fair and square but this mob was after my blood.

All three of us dipped our shoulders, rugby style, and charged past the cattle pens as the crowd poured out of the arena behind us. But there was no sign of Bill. Had they grabbed him: It was getting too hot to handle.

'Where the fuck's Bill?' I asked Neville.

'Don't worry about Bill,' he said as we clambered in the back of the white transit and the driver took off at high speed, sending mud flying off the back tyres. His walkie-talkie crackled away on the dashboard as the van careered across the field outside the barn and then out through the open farm gate. Inside, I dabbed my fight wounds with a towel and tried to stem the blood flowing from the inside of my mouth. My hands were red raw once again. I spat globs of blood into the white towel.

'What's happened to Bill?' I asked again.

Then the driver chipped in: 'He'll be alright.'

I wondered if he was having us on. We were stuck in the back of a transit van going through bandit country. I didn't argue with him.

When we reached the airfield, the driver dumped us about a hundred yards from the aeroplane in the pitch dark so we could only just make it out in the distance. The pilot and co-pilot were leaning against the fuselage, but there was no sign of anyone else.

Neville and Wayne were well twitchy and began looking around in case we were about to be ambushed. We all knew that those crazy Paddies back in the barn had lost a bucket-load of wedge by betting on their man and they might now be out for revenge.

Suddenly two pairs of blinding, fullbeam headlights appeared in the dark distance. Wayne and Neville looked at each other. That's when Neville pulled out a shooter and started waving it around. Wayne produced a knife with a twelve-inch blade.

I stood there like a sitting duck with blood soaking through the front of my white T-shirt. Neville had claret running down the side of his face from where that bottle had hit him a few minutes earlier. He started waving his gun towards the fast-approaching cars. The headlights were virtually upon us. I stepped behind my two minders. The cars got even nearer.

'Who the fuck is it?' I asked.

'Dunno,' came Neville's response. His gun was aimed straight at them.

I heard him flick the safety catch off his weapon.

The two cars slithered to a halt on the muddy field. The doors swung open and a familiar voice shouted: 'Put that fuckin' thing away.'

It was Bill and he was behaving as if we'd just come out of the local boozer and were organising a ride home.

On board I strapped in next to Wayne and Neville – the only two fellas I trusted on that entire plane. Bill stayed up front, drinking with his cronies as if he didn't have a care in the world.

Once we got to cruising altitude, Bill wandered up to us and slung mean envelope containing £5000.

'What happened back there?' I asked.

'Nothin' special,' said Bill with a grin.

'Nothin' special? It was fuckin' hairy,' I said.

'Nah, that was nothin', Son,' added Bill.

I wasn't convinced.

Neville, Wayne and myself had ourselves a few drinks on that plane trip home. I wouldn't have minded changing my pants as well! But Neville and Wayne kept me laughing all the way. They knew the score because they'd worked in the illegal fight game with Bill for years. But I felt they were more on my side than his.

When we finally touched down in Essex, all Bill said to me was: 'I'll bell you in a few days.' It was clear his only concern was his next fat pay packet, thanks to yours truly. He didn't even ask me if I was alright.

Neville and Wayne were a different story. They got me in Neville's Capri and took me to hospital to sort out a nasty wound to the back of my head. They were good fellas and I believed I'd made friends for life.

At Queen Mary's Hospital, in Stratford, the casualty department sewed me up a treat and the boys stuck with me throughout the night and even dropped me back at my flat. It was about three in the morning by the time I tip-toed in. Luckily Carole was asleep.

Next morning; I woke up late to find my pillow soaked in blood. My nose was the size of a balloon and my hands were red raw, as usual.

'What happened to you?' asked Carole.

'Had a big tear-up at the club. Punter went a bit mad.'

'You're the mad one. Who'd want a job like yours?' said Carole, dabbing at my wounds with some cotton wool soaked in hot water. If only she knew the truth.

Luckily she didn't notice the two-inch gash inside my mouth and didn't stumble across the five grand in cash still sitting in my inside jacket pocket.

I didn't show up on the building site for the next couple of days. My mouth was so sore I couldn't eat. I did a lot of thinking over that period and decided I'd never let Bill risk my life like that ever again.

CHAPTER THIRTEEN

# Fly by Night

All the aggro with that fight in Ireland left me in a bit of state. I had to face up to a few facts: I was risking ending up on a mortuary slab for the sake of a few grand in my pocket. And if there was ever to be a next time then I had to insist Bill told me more about the fight in advance.

Of course I would have coped more easily if I wasn't still bottling everything up and not telling a soul about my secret life as an illegal fighter. The strain of it was doing my head in. But at least I had my new mates Neville and Wayne. They tried to put my mind at rest by saying Bill was a trustworthy fella. But I was far from convinced.

But my biggest priority was not losing Carole under any circumstances. She was already putting me under pressure to stop working as a 'doorman' – my cover for going off training and then fighting. I told her we needed the money for our wedding and that I'd quit as soon as we actually got married. I knew she wasn't happy, but it was better than telling her the truth.

I needed enough dough to buy our own place, settle down and have kids. That was the dream. I so wanted a happy, stable life different to the one I'd had thanks to my wayward dad. If it meant taking a few on the chin and risking a beating then so be it. But was it really worth risking my life for?

With all the money pressures mounting, I let Bill talk me into taking on two more 'jobs', as he liked to call them. They were both in cages. One was in the Ipswich area of Suffolk and the other was in Birmingham. Luckily both of them were brief and victorious and I copped three-and-a-half grand for each bout. They weren't that different from my first fight in the cage and I insisted to Bill that Wayne and Neville were alongside me so at least I felt a little bit more secure.

The Ipswich fight was in another warehouse on an industrial estate. The fight in the Midlands was held in a huge underground car park near the Bullring in the centre of Birmingham. They both lasted under a minute, thanks to my opponents being old and fat. These fights also confirmed to me that Bill was raking in a lot more dough after putting thousands of quid on me in bets, as well as splitting the 'match fee' with me.

The next fight was in South London and the crowd there got really out of control when I steamrollered some local fella who looked like the England footballer Rio Ferdinand. He lasted about a minute and a half. Turned out he had a kickboxing background and the home crowd thought their man would walk it. They started banging on our van and even tried to rock it over. Neville couldn't get the motor started. I was laughing my head off for some strange reason. After winning a tough fight, a few problems with the crowd seemed like small fry. Neville and Wayne got really wound up, while Bill, as usual, was nowhere to be found.

Secrecy was the key to all these fights. At one bout, some idiot started taking pictures with a flash. Three heavies grabbed his camera, stamped on it and then stamped on this geezer's face for good measure. Wayne and Neville said that amongst the audience at those fights were a lot of senior Old Bill. Many of them were partial to a flutter and the big-time crims liked entertaining the cozzers. One time Wayne even recognised a judge in the audience because it was the same fells who'd sent him down a few years earlier. I also spotted a number of East End actors at some of the fights.

By the time my fifth fight came around Bill had bought himself a brand-new S-class Mercedes with his own personal driver. Meanwhile, I was still saving hard for my wedding to Carole. I'd be a liar if I didn't admit it niggled me that Bill was making so much dough out of me. He definitely also had a couple of other fighters on his books, but refused pointblank to even discuss them. The secretive world of the cage and illegal fighting was very convenient for Bill. It meant he could avoid all sorts of other issues.

Besides the wedding money, I'd also given Mum quite a few bob. She deserved it. She still worked at the pub and was too proud to ever ask for any money, so I'd drop a little something in her biscuit tin whenever I was round at her gaff. She never asked me where it came from. Luckily, during this run of quick fights, I didn't suffer any bad injuries or marks to my face so neither Carole nor my mum suspected what I was up to. So far so good.

I was still determined to contribute towards our wedding. Carole wanted the full works for what she saw as the most special day of her life. I'd have been happiest with a few mates at a quiet little ceremony, but you gotta let the little lady in your life have what she wants, haven't you?

As it happens, 9 May 1987 turned out to be a great day for all. The wedding ceremony itself was held in a massive old church that hadn't been used for more than two years, in the middle of the old Stratford one-way system. About four hundred people turned up, including the shadowy Bill; no doubt he saw it as a necessary duty to keep me sweet.

I'd asked him along as a 'business associate'. Bill came to the church service, but didn't show up at the party afterwards. He didn't bring his wife or anyone else and I only realised he was there when I spotted his Mercedes and driver slung up as we walked out of the church following the ceremony.

As we were posing for photos, Bill wandered over. I had a quick chat without bothering to introduce him to anyone. As we shook hands, he slipped me an envelope containing a couple of hundred quid. 'Congratulations,' was all he said before heading off through the crowd back to his Merc.

'Who s that?' Carole asked me a few seconds later. I lied. 'Boss of a club where I work.'

'Oh,' she said.

Well, it was the nearest to the truth I could manage at the time.

The only disappointment of the day was that my Uncle Pete, who was back in England, didn't show up because his car broke down. I would have liked him to see me on my biggest day. I owed him a lot in many ways.

Amazingly, my old man did make an appearance. Naturally, he had a new girlfriend in tow. The wedding reception went with a real swing thanks to a great mixture of people from all backgrounds. But ultimately, it was Carole's day. I just tried to behave myself and keep a low profile.

My new father-in-law, Jim, even told the reception in his speech: 'He's a good boy who never stops working.' Coming from him that was a compliment. If only he knew the truth. Shortly after the wedding, Jim even had the decency to come up to me and say how wrong he was about me and that I was 'alright after all'.

Just as we were about to leave for our honeymoon, Mum grabbed my hand and asked me a strange question: 'So where's all this money coming from, Carl?'

'Don't worry about it, Mum.'

'You're not goin' to get yourself in trouble are you?'

'Nah,' I tried to say it with a smile on my face, but I was worried because I didn't want her thinking I was up to no good.

Carole and me spent the first couple of nights of our honeymoon at a hotel by the sea in Clacton before setting off for the sunshine of Corfu. Carole's dad stumped up for the honeymoon, which was nice of him. I got quite a shock when I first saw all the topless girls on the beach but I soon got used to it!

It was a difficult time because I didn't like hiding the truth from Carole. One side of me felt really bad about it. But I handled it by blanking it out of my mind most of the time we were in Corfu, although Carole did catch me once or twice looking a bit thoughtful.

'What you thinkin' about Carl?'

'Nothin' special.'

What else could I say?

Once we got back to East London I tried to keep myself as busy as possible with plenty of hod-carrying work. I kept up a strict training regime, but I told myself it was for my health rather than any future fights. I even convinced myself that the £200 wedding present from Bill didn't mean I had to commit to another fight. My ultimate goal remained a happy family and home. I'd had a good run and each fight had seemed easier than the previous one, but now I wanted to put all that behind me.

In June 1987, Carole and I bought our own flat in Keogh Road, Stratford. I'd managed to steer clear of Bill ever since the wedding. He regularly called but I told him I was doing up my new home and didn't have time to do anything else. I had responsibilities now for the first time in my life. But in some ways I was leaving the door wide open. Something inside me stopped me from completely blowing out Bill. I didn't want to slam that door shut just in case there came a day when I needed him again ...

CHAPTER FOURTEEN

# Le Underground

Doing up that flat cost a lot more money than I'd expected. I was still working in the building game, but Carole's salary and mine never seemed to cover everything. Also, it was pretty relentless working on other people's homes and then coming back to do the same thing all over again in my own place.

I had quite a few restless nights thinking about my next move. Then, in the middle of 1988, I called Bill up and left a message on his answer machine. When he didn't call back I started to wonder if I'd blown it by turning him down so many times since the wedding.

Then our bank statement turned up in the post and I rang him again. This time Bill picked up after just two rings. He must have known how desperate I was, but he made no reference to my earlier call.

'There might be somethin' about for you. I'll have to make a few calls,' Bill said.

'This time I need to know more about who I'm fighting,' I said.

'Can't talk on the dog, Son. Let's have a meet.'

This time it was at a real spit 'n' sawdust tavern called The Swan, in a tough old manor near the Rotherhithe Tunnel. Bill was already in the boozer with his driver and a minder when I showed up.

Bill went a bit moody on me at first. Maybe he was punishing me for turning my back on him for so long.

'So what d'you wanna know so bad?' he said dismissively. 'If I'm gonna get back into this game I gotta know more about the opposition this time.'

'That's not on.'

'Yes it fuckin' is 'cause I gotta be better prepared than I have been in the past. One day I'll come up against a hitter who's really the business and I'll be in trouble.'

'That's not down to me, Son.'

'Just keep me posted, alright?' I paused. 'And I want my own people alongside me,' I said, knowing I was pushing my luck.

'No way.'

'Then count me out.'

'I provide the muscle, not you.'

'Just make sure Neville and Wayne are at every fight.'

Bill looked relieved when I said their names because they were already on his payroll. Looking back on it, I was playing right into his hands.

I drove home after that meet with Bill in my rusting old two-litre Cortina Ghia kidding myself that I now had a measure of control over my own destiny. With Neville and Wayne on side, maybe I'd even have a bit of a laugh as well as earn a crust.

A couple of days later Bill called up again.

Day after tomorrow.'

'What about the dough?'

Not on the phone.'

Yet again he was telling me nothing, but at least there was a fight in the air and I needed the cash badly.

Next I belled Neville and Wayne and asked them if they had any idea who I was up against. Wayne promised me he'd get back to me, soon as he heard something. Naturally, he was as good as his word.

Within half an hour, Wayne was back on the old dog and bone.

'Bring your passport, bruv.' 'Where we goin'?'

'I think they eat snails.'

'What?'

'Think about it ...'

We were off to France. Wayne also reckoned I'd walk the fight, but I wasn't sure how the hell he could be so certain.

We flew Air France to Paris – none of that cloak-and-dagger stuff at tiny airfields in wobbly planes with two rusting props. But there was no Bill on board. Instead I found myself sandwiched between my two six-foot-three-inch heavyweight friends Wayne and Neville. We must have looked a frightening threesome to all the other passengers. We even had to pull the arm rests up between us just so we could all squeeze into a row of seats together.

Sticking out like three sumo wrestlers at a garden centre

meant we, naturally, got thoroughly searched by customs at Charles de Gaulle Airport. When we finally walked out into arrivals, we bumped straight into this little garlic-breathed fella with a scrap of paper in his mitt which read WAYNE.

Our new pint-sized friend drove us off in a Citroën with blacked-out windows and, thirty minutes later, we were waltzed into the plushest hotel reception I've ever seen in my life. Bill was sitting there, cool as a cucumber, in the lobby. We all joined him.

'No muddy field filled with shamrock merchants this time?' I asked.

Bill laughed. 'Don't worry, Son. This one's in a different league.'

Bill even kept to his side of the bargain by giving me a proper pre-fight briefing. I was fighting in a cage in an underground car park beneath another big hotel just a few minutes from where we were sitting.

Just then, I noticed Wayne being handed a bulky-looking paper bag by one of Bill's other minders: Looked like a shooter just in case anything went wrong.

'You sure this one's alright?' I asked Bill.

He laughed. 'Just a little insurance, Son.'

Then Bill continued his briefing on my opponent. His height, weight and previous fights. 'He's not bad, a bit flash but you'll hammer him easy,' said Bill. How the hell could he be so sure?

A few minutes later, two French limos drew up outside the hotel and it was time for the off. One vehicle – a Citroën Pallas – was driven by Bill's regular minder. Our car was piloted by an immaculately dressed Frenchman who didn't speak a word of English. I remember he had this huge mobile phone which he used every other second for some call or other. It was certainly a bit slicker this time around. Maybe Bill was right.

It was night-time by now and I sat in the back hemmed between Neville and Wayne in a bumper-to-bumper traffic jam near the Eiffel Tower. Then we went and lost Bill's car at some lights. But luckily our man knew where he was going.

A few minutes later, our limo cruised into a car park and started twisting down a spiral roadway below ground level. We must have gone round at least six times when we were stopped by another well-dressed fella. He leant in and spoke to the driver in French, gave us a cursory glance and waved us in. I noticed the handle of a shooter in a holster under his jacket.

Then I saw the cage. It was carefully lit like something on a movie set or theatre. All around were well-dressed people, including a lot of very glamorous-looking ladies. Many of them looked like stunning catwalk models.

The cage itself was entirely on its own in a far corner of the car park. People were milling around it. Many were carrying bottles of champagne by the neck. At least a dozen men and women were snorting cocaine off the sparkling clean bonnets of a row of Mercedes and BMWs. None of them even bothered looking up as our vehicle slowly cruised through the car park.

As we came to a halt another limo slid in alongside us. A blonde woman in the back seat was scooping something from a small glass bottle and then sniffing it. More cocaine I guess. Music was blasting out of a PA system, giving the whole place an even more dramatic atmosphere. It sounded like French jazz music and was what I'd call very sexy sounds. There were even some black people swarming around, which was unusual because in most of my fights to date there had been a distinct lack of anyone who wasn't white. The smoothest-looking bookies I'd ever seen were handling all the cash with expensive leather holders under their arms. None of those old-fashioned cases with legs like I'd seen back in England.

As I got out, all heads turned towards me. Bill appeared alongside me from the other limo. 'You alright, Son?' I'd never felt more relaxed in my life, but I didn't want to admit that to Bill. 'Fine.'

I began my warm-up by stretching my body over the bonnet of the Citroen. When I looked up at the ceiling I noticed it was very high for an underground car park and the organisers had bolted extra lighting to overhead beams to improve the atmosphere.

It was only then I saw my opponent on the other side of the cage. He was kicking into the air with a bunch of flashy looking warm-up exercises. He looked like some kind of street fighter because they always use their legs like that. Silly bastard was showing off in front of a bunch of gorgeous-looking birds standing nearby, but all he was doing was giving away his trade secrets before we'd even got in the cage.

His jet-black hair was so over-slicked back, he looked like he'd just dipped his head in a bucket of olive oil. And he had a gleaming body that looked more suited to page seven of the *Sun*. Obviously, he fancied himself as a bit of a Claude Van Damme. I sized him up carefully but kept myself very low profile in comparison, which suited me just fine. He was so up his own arse I'm not sure he even noticed me. 'Look at *dat bumba clot* ["wanker" in Jamaican],' chuckled my mate Wayne, moving into full West Indian mode.

Next to me Bill handed over a wad of bank notes to a bookie

in a £1000 suit. Then he nodded towards us and said: 'Follow me, lads.'

The cage had been very carefully constructed with mesh and metal bars expertly bolted together. This time the entrance doors were taller. At least I wouldn't have to stoop so low to get in. Just then a compère started babbling in French on the PA system. Less than a minute later, he dropped his hands as we both entered the cage through our separate doorways.

'Watch his feet,' screamed Neville as he slammed shut the gate.

'*Allez!*'

It was only then that my slicked-up opponent actually looked me in the eyes. And he didn't keep it up for more than a split second.

The crowd went completely silent at first, then some of them began shouting in French.

Mr Smoothy came straight at me with a bunch of – surprise, surprise – side kicks. He completely missed me as I ducked away with an immaculate Ali shuffle to one side. Then I caught his knee with my arm and grabbed his leg so he couldn't get away. I punched him twice straight in the face and he fell backwards but I still had his leg in my hand. The crowd was getting noisier. I could tell they were annoyed I was in control. Then I let Mr Smoothy crash to the tarmac, dropped to my knees and bang, bang, straight up with my fists into his pretty little face. He went out like a light.

The crowd went hysterical. They'd all just lost a bucket-load of dough in a matter of seconds. Many of them, including some of the women, grabbed onto the mesh of the cage and peered in at us like we were wild animals in a zoo. They were trying to shout him out of his unconscious state but he remained out for the count. I stood waiting for the nod to end the fight or to have another whack at him if he woke up. Just then his manager got into the cage and crouched down to examine Mr Smoothy. Another fella then appeared who must have been a doctor.

The coked-up crowd continued rattling the cage. Bill waved me out and I headed for the door. By now the punters were rocking the cage so much it was quite tricky getting out of the door. Bill had a big Cheshire-cat grin on his old, haggard face as we moved through the crowds.

'That was a piece of fuckin' cake,' yelled Bill.

'Yeah. Too fuckin' easy,' I snapped back.

Just before we got to the limo, a blonde and a brunette appeared out of nowhere. Bill smiled and moved to one side to let them get closer to me. In broken English, one of them said to me, 'Come with us to a party.' The other one handed me a card.

'No thanks.'

'Come on. We can 'ave some fun,' said the brunette. 'Shame we can't take 'em back with us in our suitcases,' grinned Neville, who was right alongside me like a good minder.

'Here's their card,' I said. 'Be my guest.'

Truth is, when you're at an illegal fight in a strange country filled with cocaine-snorting hoods, the last thing you want is to start partying with their molls. In any case, I was a newly married man!

That night I eventually rolled home in the early hours to find Carole fast asleep. It made it all worth it when I saw her lying there. As far as she was concerned I'd been out working the door at a West End club. The next day Bill bunged me an envelope containing £6000 for that fight in Paris. Not bad for under a minute's work. I gave Neville and Wayne £500 on top of what they no doubt earned from Bill. They were worth every penny of it.

And I kept up my own limited training schedule by spending at least one hour every day in the garden using mild weights. Nothing too heavy because I didn't want to bulk up and lose my speed. Then I'd run two or three miles every day, usually around Wanstead Flats. In the middle of all this I did a lot of stretching and side bends. And I kept my muscles toned at all times. I also went to the local baths and swam up to fifty lengths and then had a session on the running machine.

On the food front, I stuck to a diet of mainly pasta, potatoes, rice and white meat, with lots of milk for the calcium. Definitely no fry-ups and no burgers.

Shortly after the France fight, I met Wayne and Neville for a beer and they let it slip that quite a number of fighters had popped their clogs at bouts organised by Bill.

'But it ain't your problem, bruv,' said Neville.

I shrugged my shoulders and tried not to look too bothered. But inside I was well upset. I never wanted anyone to die although I knew that the fighters I faced wouldn't have thought twice about finishing me off. Neville felt bad about blurting this information out. Bill had no doubt tried to keep the truth from me about the deaths because he didn't want me to be put off.

A few weeks later I confronted Bill about the whole business. He admitted he'd heard from one of his people that the other fighter I'd knocked out in my first fight had died from a brain haemorrhage. When Bill told me he patted me on the back as if to say well done for killing that poor bastard. 'Fuck off, you prat,' I snapped back at him. 'D'you think I wanted him to die?'

I was gutted when I heard about that other fella. And it could so easily have been me. Hearing about that other fighter's death made me decide I had to get out of the game. Then my younger brother Ian got me a job at a well-known hotel in the West End as a handyman. It was a full-time job and I hoped it might help keep me off the circuit now I was happily married and settled with Carole.

But it's almost as if trouble just followed me around because on my second day I bumped into a chef who I'd boxed when he was at West Ham Boys' Club. He was organising illegal fights in the basement of the hotel.

He offered me £500 to fight the following week. Everyone was in there: the managers, valets, even a few snotty guests making big bets – you name it. It turned out the hotel had been running illegal fights for two hundred years: it was as traditional as strawberries and cream. The fights were held at 6.30pm every few months. I fought another chef who specialised in pastry and – sorry about this – I gave him a right pasting inside a minute. A lot of punters made a packet by betting on me and I was given the red carpet treatment by the other staff from then on.

But having a full-time job didn't really suit my mentality and, within a couple of months, I'd quit that posh hotel up West and gone back to the building game. It was almost as if I was trying to find an excuse to fight again.

## CHAPTER FIFTEEN

# Emerald Isle

In the winter of 1988 the same old pressures started mounting yet again and I fell for another bucketload of dough being dangled in front of me by Bill. This time we flew over to Cork, in Eire, for a fight that featured the sloppiest cage I'd ever seen. Bolts were sticking out of it and some of the wire mesh hadn't even been properly smoothed down. But none of that seemed to bother the big, fat, wobbly, ginger-haired gypsy who'd been lined up to teach me a lesson. The fight took under two minutes and I came out £8000 richer.

But that bout will always stay with me for a much more sinister reason. As I was being whisked to the local airfield after the fight, the crowd of mainly farmers and gypsies ripped the cage to pieces because they'd lost so much money betting on their boy. Then they grabbed him – he was still out cold from our fight – from the floor and dragged him outside where they slung him in an old car and set fire to it. He burnt to death. That was even heavier than a fella dying inside the cage.

It shook me to the core when I heard about it from a mate of Bill's, who I happened to be speaking to some time later. It turned out Bill was desperate for me not to know what had happened to that poor bastard because he didn't want me quitting on him.

Yet again, I confronted Bill. He denied it had even happened, but I knew from the look on his face that he was lying. I now knew for certain I couldn't trust Bill to look after me. Maybe I'd end up being burned to death in a car if I lost a fight and, with it, lost Bill a load of money? No doubt one day I'd come up against a tastier operator than myself. It was just a matter of time, wasn't it?

One day I asked Neville and Wayne what they reckoned. 'Hope you wouldn't let that happen to me,' I said to them. 'No way, bruv,' they both replied. And I believed them. But Bill was my paymaster whether I liked it or not and, just so long as I needed the money, he'd be there looming over me like the grim reaper.

Away from the fight game, I remained close to my mum and brothers and sister. That meant I occasionally got called upon to sort out a few domestic problems.

Shortly after I got back from that fight in Ireland, my mum called me up in a right state. My sister Lee – who'd just turned fifteen – had run off with an older boy and she was worried sick like any good mum would be. Turned out this youth – his name was Alex – was also suspected of knocking my sis around. Now that's simply not on in my book. Any man who hits a woman or child has got it coming to them.

Lee had already been missing for an entire night and Mum

was worried she might not see her again. Lee had never been home late before, let alone spent the entire night out. So me and my brothers began our hunt for her by knocking on the door of every friend of Lee and her boyfriend. In the middle of all this, Lee phoned home and announced to Mum she was never going to come home again.

Now I have to tell you here and now that I'm very protective towards my kid sister. Us boys were brought up by our mum to look after the women in the family, no matter what. She was only a kid so we knew it was our duty to get her home.

Many of Alex's mates denied knowing anything about them, but I soon 'persuaded' them to change their minds, and it emerged on the grapevine that Lee was living with this boy in Brixton – not the sort of place anyone wants their fourteen-year-old sister to hang around. As far as I was concerned anything south of the river was foreign.

It also turned out this boy's dad was a screw at Pentonville Prison, so he wasn't exactly the most popular bloke in his street in Forest Gate. The old man had the front to tell me to fuck off when I first called round at their house. He even threatened to call the cozzers. So I retreated to reconsider my actions.

Meanwhile my dear old mum goes and gets the law involved herself. I was a bit peeved with her at first because she'd asked me to take care of things. We'd always been brought up to look after our own and not involve the police, but I guess she was worried sick about her little baby.

Then Lee put in a second phone call and says she wants to come home, but she's scared this boy might do something to her if she leaves him. It seemed like he had some kind of hold over her. I didn't like the sound of it one bit.

'But I don't want you to hurt him,' Lee told me as she sobbed down the phone.

'All we want is for you to come home. We don't want you stuck out there in Brixton,' I said, trying to be reassuring.

'Brixton?' she says.

That's when it turned out she was living just round the corner from our gaff. Anyway, less than an hour later, she came rolling in, full of tears and remorse. But I could see that boy had scared her out of her wits, which wasn't on. Lee still begged me not to hurt him. 'Just tell me where he is,' I asked. 'I need to have a chat with him.'

But Lee wouldn't tell me where I could find him so I put some feelers out in the hope of getting a fix on his location. A couple of days later we were holding a farewell party for my older brother John, who was off to live in California, when a mate knocked on the front door and said this boy Alex had just turned up at a nearby boozer called the Camden Arms. I had a quiet word with my younger brother Ian out of earshot of my mum and Lee. Then I told Mum we were going to run out for some more beers.

We got to the Camden Arms to find this kid standing outside chatting to his mates with a pint mug in his hand. Ian jumped out of the motor before I'd even parked up and laid right into him. I joined in moments later.

At least this little runt took his punishment like a man. We were careful not to go over the top. We just wanted him to get the message – don't hit Lee or any girl for that matter. After I'd decked him out with a right hook I looked down at him lying on the pavement outside the boozer and said: 'I don't want to see your face again in Forest Gate.' He left the manor shortly afterwards.

Next day, after seeing my big bruv John off at the airport, I told Mum and Lee what had happened. Lee wasn't too happy but, years later, she thanked me for what I'd done because she could have so easily destroyed her life with that young wally. That night my mum came up to me in the kitchen and whispered, 'Thanks for sorting it all out. I love you, Son.' And I knew she meant every word.

Strange thing is that this boy's family also moved off the manor soon afterwards. Might have had something to do with the fact I'd threatened to tell every ex-con in Forest Gate where that bastard lived. Screws are not popular people round there.

I've told you what happened with Lee because it's important to understand that, in the world I live in, you look after your own. It's something I've been brought up to do and it's never left me. I'd do the same for anyone in distress.

By the autumn of 1989 I'd taken a break of almost a year from the fight game simply because Bill couldn't come up with any more mugs for me to KO. No one seemed keen on spending any time in the cage with me. Funny thing is that I'd never even talked to any of my opponents. I had no idea what happened to older fighters, but I did know from Bill that no one was keen on meeting me because I was unbeaten. Suppose it's tricky trying to get some bets going if you know it's going to be a one-sided contest. Looking back on it, I don't know how I could be such a mug and not take more interest in the whole illegal fight game – especially since I was putting my life on the line every time I got in the cage.

So after a long gap without any dough, I was happy as pie when Bill came up with a £5000 pay packet for a job just up the road at Dagenham Docks. It sounded like a piece of cake. Bill told me I'd be the second of two fights on the night and insisted it was a properly organised, full-on sort of gig, so I was happy.

By now Bill was fairly open about who I was going to fight as I wanted to avoid the sort of problems I'd experienced earlier in my career. He said my opponent was a local fella and that I'd cruise it like all my previous fights. I was still working the building sites in the day and training flat out four evenings a week, so I was brimming with fitness – and confidence.

That evening, Bill and I cruised down to Dagenham Docks in his sparkling silver Merc, complete with driver and my two old muckers, Wayne and Neville. It was dark and wet by the time we turned onto the dockside right alongside the Thames, where rusting yellow and orange containers were stacked about 200 feet high. You could smell the river wafting through the car as we drove along the shiny, wet tarmac. I looked at Bill's car clock – it was 10.30 pm.

Then we turned a corner and drove down a narrow lane between two more huge stacks of containers. At the end of the lane stood at least 250 fellas. I mean real, tasty, hard cases and they were being very noisy. The cold night air was full of rasping steam. And not one woman was in sight. This was going to be a serious evening. Amongst the punters were a lot of godfather types in long Crombie coats, with gold jewellery dangling off their wrists and long, fat cigars sticking out of their big, ugly mouths.

'Watch yourself. This bloke's fit,' muttered Neville, just out of Bill's earshot as we glided to a halt. I nodded. I then spotted the cage set up on the dockside. Alongside it was the fella I presumed was my opponent. He was well built with at least a

54-inch chest. Big arms, big oak-tree legs. And wearing the traditional T-shirt and jeans.

Just then the car doors opened and me, Neville and Wayne were surrounded by six even bigger geezers. They moved with us as we walked towards the cage where my latest opponent was waiting, calmly pacing the other side.

'Go on, my son,' one old lag shouted through his clenched teeth.

'Get in there, boy.'

There was no ringmaster this time. And I knew that once we'd clambered into that cage I was on my own. My opponent came at me with a flurry of punches within what seemed like a split second, not even giving me the customary amount of time to settle. Then he kneed me sharply in the ribs. I was winded and doubled up. He followed that up with two ferocious headbutts. I was staggering all over the shop. I hadn't got one decent punch in by this stage.

Then I straightened up and went after him, quickly connecting with a handful of punches, but they didn't seem to have much effect on him. The sheer determination of this character was awesome. Everything I threw at him literally bounced off his upper body. Then he came back at me relentlessly. He was soon playing with me just to entertain the crowd. I tried to duck his firepower to give myself enough time to regain my composure but he wouldn't give me an inch.

From just outside the cage I heard Neville screaming: 'Move! Move! For fuck's sake move!'

But by this time I wasn't much better than a statue. My vision was badly blurred. My stomach was cramped. And he kept coming back and hitting me precisely on target. I was walking into his punches. My brain had slowed down and I was starting to lose all sense of co-ordination. I needed to pull something out of the bag but my nut was so scrambled my thoughts wouldn't connect to my fists. Just then he connected with a mighty right to my neck and my world went black.

Next thing I remember was coming round in the back of Wayne's rusting old purple Capri as we drove to Whipp's Cross Hospital at high speed. They later told me they thought I was about to peg it. I had no memory of anything after my opponent's right fist connected with my Adam's apple. Wayne and Neville also informed me that Bill had hot-footed it seconds after the end of the bout. Nice to know he cared so much about his so-called 'prized' fighter.

I was in a bad way that night in the back of the Capri. I couldn't move either of my arms and I was slumped up against the rear window, unable to sit up straight. My head was so swollen I looked like the elephant man. After I was checked into the hospital, I found out that my nose was busted. My ear drums were bleeding, My throat was so badly swollen by my enlarged Adam's apple that I could barely breathe. I knew my jaw was fractured. My eyes were cut and so badly puffed I could only make out the shadows of objects. My knuckles were broken, mainly because I kept missing him and smashing my fists into the wall of the cage. I had badly bruised ribs. My collar bone was fractured. Even my shins were bruised and battered.

Neville later said that my opponent had jumped all over me after I'd gone down. This was fair enough as I'd have done the same thing to him. But both Neville and Wayne thought he was out to kill me. Apparently, Bill then threw the towel in the cage, but this psycho just carried on trying to finish me off. He got a final; brutal kick to my head before being pulled off me by Neville and Wayne. They knocked him out in half a minute between them. Then they rushed back into the cage and dragged me to safety.

Back at the Whipp's Cross Hospital, Neville made out to the medics they'd found me in the street and brought me in. They said they thought I'd been beaten up in a pub brawl and claimed they'd never met me before in their lives. I was just coming round for the second time when the Old Bill turned up. My arm was strapped up. I had stitching around the eyes. As one of the coppers said, 'You look like you been hit by a train, son.'

Naturally, the law wanted to know what had happened. But they didn't push me too hard on the matter because they knew I wouldn't tell 'em much. When the doctors gave me a head scan they spotted that plastic plate from the iron bar attack which had ruined my boxing career. They knew I was a scrapper. But I was more worried about the bed baths the nurses gave me twice a day!

The docs did a great job bending my three bottom front teeth back into place. They were hanging out of their sockets. Then they stitched up the inside of my mouth. It was bloody painful.

I ended up spending three days in hospital. A really sweet nurse took pity on me and phoned Carole and my mum to tell them where I was. I asked her to tell them I'd been in an accident. I could barely speak a word when Carole showed up at the hospital with Mum, who waited outside while Carole came in first. I told her I'd got into a fight outside the club where I worked the door. But I could see in her eyes that she didn't fully believe me.

Funny thing is that Carole didn't push me on what really happened. That's just not her style. Instead, she gave me a hug and made it clear she was just relieved I was still in one piece. Then she burst into tears on my shoulder. It hurt like hell when she leaned on me but I didn't care. I was just glad to have her there. I had to stop the fight game before it drove a wedge between us. I didn't want to risk losing Carole for ever.

Then Mum came in and was soon sobbing her eyes out. How could I do this to the two most important people in my life? Was I sick in the head to think I could get away with it all? 'My baby. My baby,' Mum kept sobbing over and over. I felt terrible putting them through all this.

The next day Bill turned up at my bedside to bung me my £1800 loser's fee. I'd have copped £6000 if I'd won. He asked me why I thought I'd lost. 'I dunno,' I replied through my broken teeth and torn-up mouth. I just wanted him to fuck off and leave me alone.

Bill tried to act like he cared. Then he went and ruined it by asking me to call him in a couple of weeks' time. The last thing on my mind was a return to the cage. I just turned over and pretended I'd fallen asleep so that he'd leave me in peace.

As soon as I got home from hospital, Carole and me started rowing really badly. Looking back on it, she had every right to be so pissed off with me. She knew I was up to no good but I wouldn't tell her the truth.

Carole begged me to give up the door work and I promised I would. But I didn't really know if I could stick to that promise.

'Everything'll be alright. You'll see. I'll change. I promise I will,' I told her. But I wasn't sure if I meant every word of it.

We had a quiet Christmas that year. Carole went everywhere with me. She was paranoid I'd head off back up west to the 'club' where I'd got my last beating. How could I treat her like this?

About a month or so after I got out of hospital, Bill called up and insisted I bring Carole to a dinner dance he was organising at the Room At The Top club, in Ilford. There were tables with set places and more than half the crowd were in dicky bows and black dinner jackets. We were on a table with a number of old-time faces, including a friendly Irish bloke called Kenny. He homed in on me almost immediately after I sat down.

Kenny was at least six feet tall, and very thin with shoulder-length hair cut like Kevin Keegan's when he was at Liverpool and FC Hamburg. He must have been in his late forties with sharp, chiselled features and brown eyes. He walked with a limp and had on lots of jewellery, bracelets and gold chains. He had absolutely no style and looked like a seventies fashion victim. His soft Irish accent made you think he was a laid-back kind of fella, but a nasty one-inch scar on his chin seemed to tell another story.

Kenny told me he sold used cars.

'Bill says you've done a lot of jobs with him,' he said, right in front of Carole, who was earwigging every word of our conversation.

'Yeah,' I replied, conscious that Carole was close by. 'But I've given all that up now.'

'Let's have a chat later at the bar,' muttered Kenny, more out of Carole's range.

A couple of hours later – after the speeches and the dinner were over – this fella Kenny appeared alongside me at the bar as promised. And he came straight to the point.

'I've got a proposition,' he said in his soft Irish brogue. 'More money than you could imagine.'

'Not interested,' I snapped back with a dry smile.

'You sure?'

'Abso-fuckin-lootly.'

'It's a very special job in Vegas.'

'I said no way.'

'Well, if you ever go Stateside, let me know.'

And I meant it at that moment. I had no intention of losing Carole or my life. The fight game was over. The risks were too high. I'd almost died barely a month earlier. I reckoned it was a sign from above, to get out while I still had my life intact. I turned and walked from Kenny straight back to Carole at the table. She'd hated every minute of the dinner dance. It just wasn't her scene being stuck on a table, talking to a bunch of gangsters' molls. I also knew she'd sensed my unhappiness. A few minutes later we got up and said our goodbyes. But just as I shook Kenny's hand he slipped a card into my palm. I said nothing.

On the way out Carole asked me: 'What was that all about with that bloke Kenny?'

'Just a work thing, babe.'

What sort of work?'

'Buildin' stuff.'

I'm sure she didn't believe a word I was saying.

Within weeks of meeting Kenny, another familiar problem appeared on the horizon: I was skint yet again. The recession was kicking into gear and work in the building trade was getting harder and harder to come by. But I'd made my decision not to fight and for the moment I had to stick to that.

Then me and Carole decided that perhaps we'd head out to Australia where Carole had some old school friends. We were both worried about our cash-flow problem. Heading for a new life might be the answer, although I'd naturally miss my family. I'd heard it wasn't that hard to get building work there, and anything was better than rotting away in East London.

I even suggested to Carole that we pop into Los Angeles on the way and see my older bruv, John, who'd moved out there a couple of years earlier. In the back of my mind were Kenny's words at that dinner dance. 'If you're ever in America, Son, give me a call.'

Back in East London my reputation as a hardnut was well known. One woman approached me in my local boozer and asked me to kill her husband – I laughed at her because that's just not my game – but if he ever turns up dead in the near future I'll certainly know who paid for it! I've also solved a few domestic disputes when blokes have been hitting their girlfriends or wives.

And then there's the scourge of our society: drugs. One lady neighbour of my mum's came knocking on her door when I was round for Sunday lunch one time. She was in a right state, tears rolling down her cheeks. She said a bunch of local crack dealers had moved into an empty council house round the corner and her fourteen-year-old boy had been hanging round with them and was now hooked on crack. Fourteen years old – that's totally out of order. The lady says that her boy's now so addicted to crack that he's out thieving to pay for his habit and she's scared he'll end up inside if he's not careful. Only the previous day this kid had nicked his own mum's telly to get enough money for drugs.

'I don't want you to hurt him but can you sort it out, please?' she asked me.

'I'll give it a go,' I replied. Mum looked on proudly because she knew that I'd get it sorted.

I really felt for this poor lady. She was worried out of her mind and no-one deserves that sort of stress in their lives. She'd been friends with Mum for years and we both knew exactly what she was going through.

That night I got hold of a couple of mates and we headed round to the crack den. Two of us made out we were trying to score drugs when we knocked on the door.

'Any chance of some gear?' I asked through the door to a bloke with an African accent.

'Only one can come in,' was the reply.

As the door opened, I threw one of my finest left-handers and he went down like a sack of dog shit. I walked over his body and then we walked half way up the stairs to where we could hear more people on the first floor. Then I stopped and went back and grabbed the semi-conscious 'doorman', stood him up and put him in front of us as a shield in case the others were armed, which is often the case. 'Come on you fucker,' I said to the doorman. 'We're goin' upstairs.'

They must have heard us because two younger blokes – one white and one black – came out of a door on the first floor and appeared at the top of the stairs. I shoved the doorman right in their path and produced the bats me and my mate had been carrying as weapons. It didn't take them long to get the message. 'We don't want to see you lot round these parts no more. Scram!' None of them said a word.

'If I see you again I'll kill you. This is just a taste of what's to come. Comprendo?'

I could see from the looks on their faces that they were scared shitless. We turned and walked out. Then I went to look for that fourteen-year-old boy back at his mum's house round the corner.

'Is he in?' I asked her when she answered the door.

'Yeah, come in.'

'I need to tell him what's happened to his mates.'

The kid was in the front room watching TV – his mum had bought a new one on the HP. He had no idea who I was. I told him what I'd just done to the dealers and what I'd do to him if he ever thieved off his mum again. 'Now empty your pockets,' I ordered.

He pulled out £50 in cash. He'd obviously nicked something earlier that day and was planning another visit to the crack den. By now he was shaking like a leaf. I raised my voice even louder and looked really angrily at him. Then I switched to my most menacing look. It was the only way to deal with him. 'That shit'll kill you. You'll end up like all the other silly fuckers round here – dead in the gutter. Do you hear me?'

The kid nodded his head so hard I thought it'd snap off at the hinges. Then he burst into tears. Next door his mum was crying in the kitchen. It was a very sad sight. But it had to be done.

I just kept saying over and over, 'Are you listenin' to what I'm sayin'?'

He nodded.

'D'you love your mum?' He nodded again.

'Well, now you gotta prove it.'

I left them both cuddling in the kitchen. I'd done my bit. I could hear them still crying as I quietly closed their front door behind me. He was saying to her over and over, 'I do love you, Mum, I do love you, Mum, I do love you, Mum.'

A couple of days later, the same woman came knocking on Mum's door again. 'He's been good. He's got himself a paper round,' she told us. She leant up and kissed me on the cheek. 'Thank you.' That was it. There was no need to ever talk about it again.

CHAPTER SIXTEEN

# Kenny in the Middle

I knew it was a crazy move, but I picked up the phone and called Kenny a few days later. I told him all about our plans to go abroad and how we were popping into LA on the way through to Australia.

'So what sort of money we talkin' about?' I asked.

'A lot,' answered Kenny.

Anything that would keep us going while we settled in Oz was worth a punt.

I met Kenny a few days later in a pub on Soho Square in the West End. I remember it well because I didn't often go up west and I had a hell of a time finding it! When I arrived at the boozer a few minutes late, Kenny was sitting at a corner table, sipping a gin and tonic with a mate he told to get lost when I sat down next to him.

Kenny then asked me my travel plans all over again. I

repeated that Carole and me were dropping in on my brother in LA and then heading out to Australia.

'That could work very well for me,' said Kenny in his soft Irish voice. 'I know some promoters in the States and Australia.'

'What?' I asked quizzically. 'They do that kinda thing out there, too?'

'Where d'you think the cage came from in the first place?' asked Kenny.

Then he gave me a new phone number and told me to call him when I'd firmed up my travel plans. I felt a twinge of guilt as I left the pub that evening, but we needed the extra money if we were going to start a new life in a foreign land.

Carole and I flew British Airways to LA a couple of weeks later. We stayed with my brother John and his wife Michelle at their apartment in Santa Monica, right slap bang alongside the Pacific Ocean. John's a good-looking, slim fella with dark hair and brown eyes like our mum's. He's football mad and very boisterous. He also loves a good laugh and always seems happy. I was well jealous of my bruv's life out there in the sunshine. Everything in LA seemed half the price it was back in London. It was the sort of life I hoped we'd find in Australia.

After a couple of days, I bowed to temptation and called the phone number in nearby Venice Beach that had been given to me by Kenny just before we left England. He answered on the second ring. It was almost as if he'd been sitting by the phone waiting for me to call.

Kenny sounded cool as a cucumber and totally up for getting me a fight. We arranged a meet for later that day. I put the phone down, feeling a mixture of fear, guilt and outright excitement. But this time I decided I had to stop bottling it all up, otherwise I'd end up making the sort of mistakes that could cost me my life.

So as me and my bruv breezed down Wilshire Boulevard in his old Cadillac convertible, I said to him, 'I'm not here just to see you. I've got a money spinner on the go. Could be a good earner for you. But we can't tell the girls.'

John laughed. 'What you gonna do, Carl? Rob a bank?'

'It'll all come clear when we go and see this mate of mine called Kenny.'

I wanted John to be my trainer and come with me everywhere. I also needed him to provide my alibi to Carole and Michelle. That night, before meeting Kenny, we told them we were going for a beer. It was the perfect excuse. The first of many.

We met Kenny in a small bar on Muscle Beach, Venice, where all the weight-lifters flash their torsos in a couple of open-air gyms. Kenny said the fight would be in an LA car-park – or parking lot as they call them out there. He also said the fight was booked up for two nights' time. I had to make the decision there and then. I went for it.

After saying our farewells to Kenny, me and John retired to an English-run bar in nearby Santa Monica and I told him everything about the previous fights; about Bill; about the fella who died; about the Irish bloke who got roasted; and of course about the docklands opponent who nearly killed me. At the end of it John said to me: 'You must be fuckin' mad.'

But, despite his concern, I knew he'd stick by me. Not only were we close brothers prepared to help each other out at the drop of a hat, but I knew he was a bit strapped for cash at the time as Michelle had just had a baby. Over the next couple of days I completely laid off the booze. Carole soon got suspicious, so I started carrying a bottle of beer with me, then slipping it to John who'd swig it and give it back. We agreed to tell the girls that on the night of the actual fight we were planning a heavy evening out to talk about the old days. After all, we were two close brothers who hadn't seen much of each other in ages.

When the night of the fight finally arrived, John drove me to Venice where we met Kenny, whom we followed out to a big hotel near LA Airport, known to everyone as LAX, just a couple of miles east on the freeway. John was bricking it even more than me by this stage. Every time a jet came thundering a few hundred feet overhead, he jumped out of his skin. I tried to reassure him that it'd all be fine and we'd earn a decent wedge for no more than a couple of minutes' work.

'But what if this other fells is a bit tasty?' asked John anxiously.

'I'll be fine, big bruv. I'll be just fine,' I answered. I had to put on a front for my brother. I didn't want him cracking up on me before we'd even got to the venue.

We dumped John's old banger a couple of blocks from the parking lot where the fight was to be held. Arriving in a $250 rust heap wouldn't have done my reputation any good. So we got in Kenny's shiny black Lincoln Continental alongside two English minders. They didn't say a word and they didn't look in the same league as Wayne and Neville.

As we glided into the parking lot entrance, a bunch of flashy-looking motors were lining up ahead of us. We drove up at least two floors before Kenny turned to me in the back seat.

'You okay, Son?'

'Yeah. Keep an eye on my big bruv here and make sure he doesn't get too excited.'

I poked John in the ribs and he put on a bit of smile for me. Then I asked Kenny about my opponent.

'He's just some short-arsed Mexican kid,' he said. 'You'll make mincemeat of him.'

Just then the Lincoln levelled up as we drove into the actual venue which was carefully lit up with huge lamps on adjustable legs, like they have on movie sets. There was a compère in a maroon velvet jacket with a mike in his hand standing near the cage, which glistened under a multi-coloured array of different light filters. Just then another jet thundered overhead, which certainly added to the eerie atmosphere.

I felt a bit underdressed in my jeans and t-shirt, especially when I got a first glance at my opponent. He was dressed more like a traditional boxer with tassels on a flash pair of white leather boots. His hands were taped just like a boxer but without any gloves being added. But what really struck me was that he was only about five-feet-six-inches tall, although he was built like a squat brick shithouse.

This fighter was definitely quite a lot older than me, but he was bouncing around just outside the cage like Roberto Duran performing for the crowd. His sweaty Latino trainer then started slapping him across the face, trying to psyche him up.

Meanwhile Kenny's Lincoln glided to a halt alongside a couple of cars that looked longer than most bungalows. As I got out, two or three Mafia types slapped me on the back. I thought they were just trying to soften me up. But what really caught my eye was the mix of people at that event. They weren't all gangster types; there were a lot of what I'd call rich yuppies, in their early-to-mid-thirties, with glamorous-looking women on their arms.

I even recognised a couple of Hollywood stars in amongst them, including one Oscar winner who'd been in and out of the news in recent years because of his dodgy lovelife. They were all acting as if the entire event was as normal as apple pie.

Then the compère strolled inside the cage. Moments later, he began telling the audience over his PA system about the two fighters. He even referred to me as the 'English Bulldog'. I've never been keen on nicknames and I wasn't happy to hear anything being said that even vaguely helped identify me.

That was when I realised Kenny operated in a very different way to Bill. Normally by this stage; Bill would have been chatting to me and reassuring me. Not Kenny; he was more interested in slapping a load of wedge into the greasy palm of a fat Danny DeVito lookalike, whom I presumed was a bookie.

Meanwhile, my big bruv John stood there with his hand resting reassuringly on my shoulder as we started walking towards the cage. Trouble was, his hand was shaking like a leaf. 'Calm down, bruv. You'll be alright,' I said to him with a wink and a nod; although I suppose he should have been the one saying that to me.

Then the compère started up again: 'Time for the fight to commence. Will both fighters please enter the cage: 'The Mexican was bouncing around like a pit bull terrier on speed. He even took up a stance like a proper fighter, which seemed a bit strange to me, but I didn't have time to question the rules. I stooped down and got into the cage at exactly the same time as my opponent. Our eyes met for a split second.

We both instantly moved at high speed towards each other. I

caught him first with three fast shots to the head. He hit back with two sturdy punches to the body. Then I putted him right in the temple. It obviously shocked him, and the audience, who started hissing and booing. He wobbled on his pins so I kneed him in the head and down he went. Next he tried to scramble straight back on his feet and I caught him with a hefty punch on the back of the neck. He crumpled onto the deck. This time he was out like a light. I aimed a kick into his body just to make sure he wasn't having me on.

Then I gently stabbed my foot into his ribs twice to see if he'd get up. That's when a bottle of water was thrown into the cage which was the Yanks' way of throwing in the towel. I raised my arms in victory but the boos and hisses were now so much louder I could only just make out the Jumbo flying overhead. Can't say I cared. My confidence was sky high. I felt on top of the world. I didn't give a toss about a load of verbals from a bunch of American yuppies.

'Fix,' one blond-haired bloke yelled right at me through the cage.

Then came a pathetic chorus of 'Fix. Fix. Fix. Fix.'

As I climbed out of the cage, I caught a broad grin on Kenny's face. He moved alongside me and slipped a fat envelope into my hand. It contained $10,000. I was well chuffed and about to say thanks when he disappeared in the opposite direction. Obviously I was just another piece of meat to him.

At least that dough would set me and Carole up for the first couple of months in Australia and I'd barely got a scratch in the process. I bunged brother John $2000 as we drove home in his rust-bucket. He was over the moon.

The very next day, we met Kenny for a drink in that same bar on Venice Beach. He was on a real high. No doubt he'd earned tens of thousands of dollars by gambling on me the previous night. 'I know some good fight people in Australia,' he said and gave me a number in Sydney to call. 'If we firm something up I'll fly over,' added Kenny. He was obviously a big worldwide player, on a different level to Bill.

The cage had become the most important earner in my life. I was in it hook, line and sinker. It had given me the potential to earn a fortune thousands of miles from home. I was on top of the world. I couldn't wait to get cracking again. The scene was set.

## CHAPTER SEVENTEEN

# Down Under

There's no denying that getting to Australia with a good few thousand bucks burning a hole in my pocket helped me and Carole settle down more easily. I rested up for the following three months, and Carole and I got on really well. I even got myself a building job in the Melbourne suburb of Richmond, and we stayed at the nearby home of one of Carole's oldest mates.

But when the dough started running low, I couldn't stop myself from calling up Kenny's Australian fight contact. He turned out to be an Italian called Vincenzi, who I called Vinnie from the moment we met. Vinnie's job was to fix up the fight before Kenny swarmed in to grab all the glory – and the cash. Vinnie warned me that this time there would be no cage. The only other thing I knew was that I would be fighting an Aussie and that he was a very tasty operator. That's what Vinnie reckoned anyway.

Kenny appeared on the scene a few days before the fight. It was starting to dawn on me that he really was an extremely wealthy bloke because he even had his own apartment in Melbourne. Kenny wore even more jewellery than usual and he'd started speaking in an increasingly strong Irish/American accent. It was almost as if he adapted it for people in America and Australia. Strange, really, because he'd seemed straight Irish when we'd first met in London.

Kenny reckoned the Aussies were good to deal with 'because they're so fuckin' thick-skinned.' It was only a lot later that I realised the significance of what he was saying.

On the night of my first Oz fight, Vinnie drove me to the venue in his Nissan Patrol. I felt fit and strong because Carole and I had been training at a gym in Melbourne virtually every day of the week. Of course she had no idea I was prepping a fight.

This time the fight was held in a furniture warehouse at an industrial estate on the outskirts of Melbourne. It had a roped-off ring with eight barrels, so it ended up being the same shape as a fifty-pence piece.

There were lots of Italians and Greeks in the audience. They looked like smartly dressed business types but I guess a lot of them were villains. There were a lot of four-wheel drives on display. I was dressed in my usual 'uniform' of tight T-shirt and jeans. Kenny appeared briefly but stayed firmly in the background most of the time.

The crowd circled the entire ring, and the lights were so bright they made the interior of the warehouse steaming hot. Naturally, my Aussie opponent got a load of applause, while the Pom (that was me) got booed from the moment I emerged from Vinnie's jeep. My opponent must have been about six-feet-one or two. He looked like a real bushman, complete with a hat, jeans, T-shirt and Blundstone boots, similar to what we call Chelsea boots or jodhpurs back in the East End. He had a crooked, broken nose and was standing there in the ring with his thumbs hooked in his front pockets, which made him look like a right plonker. But, most significantly, his beer belly was protruding over his hands. That was all I needed to see to believe I'd crush him.

I couldn't have been more wrong. This character kept me very busy for the first three minutes, which was already longer than any of my fights had ever lasted. He was a good scrapper and he and I even exchanged mind-blowing head-butts. Then he lashed out at me with a series of vicious kicks to the shins that really hurt: before he caught my knee and I went tumbling to the floor. I still have the mark where he hit me to this day.

But as I bounced up from the floor, I decided it was time to play the fight by my rules. He came down close on me and tried to pull me up by the head. That was when I bit a chunk out of his lip and spat it on the floor. It was an animal instinct sort of thing. I don't know why I did it but I did. It certainly shocked him because he froze in mid air.

The audience went crazy when I did that. One spectator sprang out of the crowd into the ring and punched me twice on the back of the head before he was dragged away. And I can tell you now, he knew what he was doing because those punches really hurt. Bedlam exploded all around me. The crowd had lost it.

Then I noticed Vinnie elbowing two spectators in the face. Meanwhile, I carried on laying into my Aussie opponent who was bleeding profusely from his lip wound. It was getting really nasty. I kicked out viciously at the Aussie and then he started muttering something under his breath. 'Cunt. Cunt. Cunt.'

All that did was encourage me to catch him with a sharp flurry of punches before he fell backwards onto the floor. I pummelled his face as he went down, specifically targeting his eyes and nose. Over and over. Over and over.

Just then, two sets of hands grabbed me and pulled me off him and threw me to the floor. Everything became a blur. Vinnie appeared and pulled me to my feet. I almost hit him because I didn't know who he was at first. 'It's me. It's me. Let's get the fuck outta here.'

I was in bad shape after a vicious battle that lasted more than five minutes. Just then the compère grabs my arm and hoists it high. I'm the winner. I'm the winner. What the hell is going on? No time to celebrate. Got to get the fuck outta there.

And the punters continued going AWOL. Bottles rained down into the ring. We just made it through the crowd, many of whom were throwing punches in our direction. As we scrambled into Vinnie's Nissan Patrol, they started kicking the door panels. The noise was more frightening than anything else. A mob of them were rocking the car backwards and forwards. If it had been a Fiesta, they'd have toppled it over in seconds. This was fucking hairy stuff.

As Vinnie tried to reverse out of the chaos, I'll swear I heard a thud as if we drove over something or somebody. It might well have been a body but we didn't stop to ask. Once out of the warehouse, I looked behind us and saw Kenny following in another car. There were other motors behind him trying to ram his vehicle. The bedlam was far from over.

Outside, two vans tried to ram us off the road as we careered round the narrow streets of the industrial estate. When one vehicle came alongside us, I ducked because I thought I spotted a shooter in some idiot's hand. I don't know if I was right because I wasn't going to stop to have a proper look!

We finally lost the last of them about fifteen minutes later. Shortly afterwards, Kenny flashed us to pull over. I threw a right moody at him. 'There was no fuckin'protection. Anything could have happened back there.'

'It was fine,' Kenny shrugged, as if nothing had even happened. But this time his charming Irish brogue wasn't going to be enough to calm me down.

'Fuck you, Kenny. You put all our lives on the line back there – and you bloody know it.'

'Don't talk shit,' Kenny bit back. I was outraged that he could throw such a bare-faced lie.

'I'll never fight for you again. D'you hear me?'

I felt like decking him on the spot for taking the piss.

But he still had the front to come back at me. 'I'll phone you.'

'Don't fuckin' bother,' I screamed back. Kenny was a toerag. He knew it and I knew it.

Back home that night Carole erupted when she saw the state of my face. 'This can't be another pub fight, Carl. What the hell're you doing? What's going on? You gotta tell me.' But I carried on lying. I tried to calm her down. I told her I loved her, but none of it worked this time. She'd had enough and was about to go walkabout for good. She wanted out of Oz and our marriage. How could I have allowed it to get to this?

I was so fucking angry with myself. I hadn't expected to get so badly beaten up. I thought it'd be another walk-over. I was lucky to win and I knew it. I should have gone to hospital and had myself checked out, but I'd wanted Carole to believe I wasn't that badly hurt. I'd even pushed my own crooked teeth back into place to try and look as normal as possible when I got home. But now I was getting everything I deserved.

Me and Carole talked long into that night. Of course she was steaming mad with me and she had every right to be. But I still didn't have the bottle to tell her the truth. She thought I was a punch-happy, violent drunk who couldn't be trusted to go out for a beer without having a tear-up. 'What sort of person am I married to?' she screamed at me at one stage. 'I'm not sure I even know the real you.'

I was desperate to hang onto Carole. I told her we'd go touring Oz for the next three months. At least that would keep me out of trouble for a bit. 'You mean it?' she asked. "Course I do,' I said.

A week later I was paid 11,000 Australian dollars (about £4000) by Vinnie, who was a good bloke with a lot of bottle. I respected him. Once I'd got the money, Carole and me set off and did the lot: we went to the Great Barrier Reef, got stuck in some floods, saw Ayers Rock. And it was all achieved in a rust-bucket of a Mark Three Cortina that I bought for $500 or £200.

That trip was a marriage saver for us. Carole calmed down and started to trust me again. You could say we fell back in love with each other again. And being totally out of contact with Kenny made me feel a whole lot better. He was the equivalent of a drug dealer to me. If I didn't think or talk to anyone about him, then perhaps he'd just go away for ever.

Eventually we drove back into the big metropolis of Sydney.

We'd blown all those hard-earned Aussie dollars but I wasn't going to be tempted. Or was I?

I'd always kept the number of the local fight fixer ... just in case of a rainy day. It was easy money and the painful memories of how I almost went belly-up in that last fight were already fading. You do what you do best in life, don't you? And I was a good fighter. It had to be done. I'd kept fit throughout that break with Carole. I was ready.

So I called the fixer, Colin, whose number had been given to me by Vinnie. This time Kenny wasn't involved and surprise, surprise, the money was better: 22,000 Aussie smackeroos. Colin warned me it would be a tough fight. The venue was a huge warehouse out in the middle of nowhere, about fifty miles from Melbourne. My opponent was a massive rugby-forward type and I won it after about four minutes of hard graft. Word had spread amongst the local criminal fraternity and there were faces laying huge bets, so it was obvious the cage was popular down under. Me and Carole would be able to live off the dough for months. And although Carole might not appreciate it, I'd done us both a favour. This time I explained away my injuries by claiming I'd fallen off a wall while hod-carrying. Carole accepted the story much better than if I'd gone and told her I'd had another tear-up in a pub. With no Kenny on the scene my money had shot up. This had to be a lesson for me. Now I knew for certain he was a lying piece of shit. There was no doubt he was taking more than a 60:40 cut of the fight fee, not to mention all the dough he was winning by placing bets on me. I reckon he was copping at least £100,000 a fight, the slimy bastard.

Carole and me settled in Melbourne again and rented a trailer in a caravan park. We were happy and content. We went out everywhere together. She didn't take her eyes off me for a minute. We had lots of nice new mates, and for a while life was sweet.

Now, I don't want my story to get predictable but if you cut to three months later I'm skint yet again. Surprise, surprise. There wasn't as much building work around as I'd been led to believe and we lived the good life without really worrying about tomorrow. But this time our visa was about to run out so Carole and I decided we'd had enough of Oz and we'd head back to East London. I called my big bruv John up in LA and said we might be dropping in on him soon en route to England.

Then I went and did it all over again: I rang Kenny. Now you may be asking why the hell did I do it when I knew he was a lying, thieving bastard, but if I told you I was hooked – and in need of money – would that make it any better?

Kenny was naturally delighted. I could hear the dollar signs clicking as he spoke in that gentle lilting Irish voice of his. 'As it happens, there's a fight over here soon if you're interested.' I hesitated for the shortest split second of my life. Here we go again.

Less than a week later we flew into LAX. John was at the airport to greet us with some bad news: Mum's house in Forest Gate had burned down in a fire caused by an electrical fault. There was no insurance cover and everything was destroyed: if it wasn't smoke-damaged it was burned to a crisp. But at least Mum, Lee and my kid brother Ian were unhurt.

I wanted to forget the fight and head straight back to London but I'd already committed to Kenny and knew I'd never be able to fight again if I let him down. It would only delay our journey by forty-eight hours and then there was the money.

Naturally, Carole was a bit suspicious about why I hadn't wanted to get on the first flight home. She had a dig at me about it and that left me feeling very guilty. Then she started getting very tetchy with me. 'Is there someone here you want to see?' she asked me one morning after breakfast. 'Have you got a girl here?' I couldn't tell her his name was Kenny and he was about to pay me to risk my life by walking into a cage with a homicidal maniac.

'Come on, Carl. I wanna know or else there's no point in us being married.' Bloody hell, I thought to myself. She thinks I've got some bird tucked up here. What the hell am I going to do? The last thing I wanted to do was hurt Carole in this way. Nothing was worth that.

That's when it dawned on me I had no choice in the matter. I had to tell her the whole truth – well at least part of it. 'I got something to tell you,' I said. Carole naturally thought I was about to say I'd met someone and was doing a runner. When I told her I'd been offered a one-off prize fight, she sighed with relief because it wasn't anywhere near as serious as she had feared. Of course I didn't fill her in on the other fights for the moment.

'We need the money, Carole,' I added after explaining the situation.

'Where d'you meet these kind of people in the first place?' asked Carole.

Good question. I backpedalled and decided to blame it on

John. That's what brothers are for, aren't they? 'It's only a prize fight. Nothin' dangerous, babe. Just a boxing match.'

'Yeah, right,' she snapped back, arms folded in a matronly manner. She eased up a bit when I told her that I'd earn thousands and it would help us start afresh in England. But women always know when something's not right. They've got an instinct for the truth. I learned that with my mum and I knew that was the case with Carole. But I couldn't tell her the full truth – not yet anyway.

I'm just going to get through this one and then that's it, I thought to myself. No more fights after this. As Carole would say, 'Yeah, right.'

## CHAPTER EIGHTEEN

# Leaving Las Vegas

Twenty-four hours later, big bruv John and I were flying to Vegas for a fight that Kenny assured me would be a walkover. This time, John was a lot calmer than at the previous fight in that LA parking lot. Kenny was at Vegas airport to meet us in a stretch limo. He said I was featuring in one of at least three fights. I hated Vegas from the first moment I clapped eyes on it. Lots of plastic, fake palm trees, fake tits, fake buildings, fake people. The whole place was a sham stuck in the middle of the desert to make sure it never got too near to civilization.

The contest was located in a massive hall behind one of Vegas's largest casinos. But I wasn't really thinking about the fight at all. My mind was on my dear old mum back in East London, without a home or a brass farthing to her name after that fire. Hopefully I'd be able to bung her a few bob after this fight.

I was also a bit concerned that Carole might up and run before I got back to LA. She was far from happy with what I'd been up to. Perhaps I should never have told her about the fight game in the first place?

The stretch limo dropped us at the entrance to the hallway in a massive open-air car park and, when we walked in, it looked like yet another film set. The cage was brightly and carefully lit for maximum effect. Daggers of light bounced off the glistening mesh framework. There must have been at least 300 people milling around. Most of them were young, fat-cat yuppie types in expensive yet casual gear, dripping with Cartier and Rolexes.

Me, John and Kenny sat back and watched the first two fights without anyone even sussing out I was one of the scrappers. The first bout was between a couple of good old-fashioned thumpers, but the second was like a lesson in kick boxing. It was slick but unconvincing – a bit like Las Vegas itself. I wasn't impressed.

I started warming up just before the end of the second fight. John was twitching so much, I snapped at him to cut it out because it was starting to make me feel like shit. I needed to psyche myself up. And I was far from focused on the job at hand.

Then I spotted my opponent warming up on the other side of the cage. He was a big Mexican, much taller than that one back in LA, and he looked trim and fit. Then the compère announced over the PA system: 'Ladies and Gentlemen, we present the London Limey, winner in LA recently, versus the winner of four straight Vegas fights. This promises to be one helluva battle.'

London Limey, who thought that one up? I was irritated

**196**

because I'd told Kenny to cut out the nicknames during the last battle in LA. I still didn't like the crowd knowing where I was from because that might help give away my true identity.

Opposite me, the fit Mexican was trying to wind me up. He couldn't take his eyes off me. I tried my hardest to give him a cold, hard stare back but I didn't really have my heart in it. I just wasn't all there. I wanted to be back in East London, helping out my family.

As soon as I climbed into the cage that afternoon, I went straight for my opponent. Get it over quickly, I kept thinking to myself. It's gotta be the only way. It was a complete disaster; I ran straight into a flurry of punches and kicks that demolished me in a matter of seconds.

For the second time in my career as an illegal fighter, my world went black. I was out cold. Sparko. Finito. End of contest. Not even half a minute had passed.

I was just starting to come round when my seriously blurred vision caught sight of a towel being thrown into the cage. I got to my hands and knees. Then I stopped and collapsed back on the floor, head in hands. It was all over virtually before it had begun. Luckily for me my opponent didn't finish me off with his feet.

Kenny's two hefty British minders and my brother John dragged me out of the cage like a piece of dead meat. 'Don't worry, bruv. You'll be alright,' said John, but he didn't sound very convincing. Just then I heard Kenny's voice: 'Get him in the limo and straight to the airport.'

The purse for that pasting was a measly $2500. It wasn't worth a cent of it. I couldn't even afford to give John any dough and if it hadn't been for him I'm not sure we'd have got out of there in one piece.

He virtually carried me through Vegas airport and onto the plane. No one else would have shown such loving care and attention – certainly not Kenny. Once on board that plane, I had only one thing on my mind: Carole. 'She's gonna kill me, John. My marriage is finished. She'll never forgive me. Please get me home, big bruv.'

We got a taxi from LAX to John's apartment in Santa Monica. I'd just about pulled myself together as I hobbled through the front door, my face blown up like a pineapple, complete with two crimson shiners.

Carole flung her arms around me and burst into floods of tears. I felt like shit. I'd nearly lost my life out there. 'Let's get home, babe,' I muttered into her ear as we stood there in the hallway hugging for at least ten minutes. Two days later we touched down at Heathrow.

## CHAPTER NINETEEN

# Low Profile

From 1991 to 1993 I steered totally clear of the cage by getting plenty of work in the building game. I'd promised Carole after that disastrous last bout in Vegas that I'd never do it again. Naturally, Carole kept a close eye on me at all times in case I got tempted. But our main priority was to start a family.

Not that it was easy adjusting back to East London. We spent the first year after our return living with Carole's mum because our flat was rented out and we needed the income in order to survive. The following year we moved in with my mum, which was quite tricky for Carole. But we got through it in the end – although sometimes we found ourselves under a lot of heavy pressure because of the obvious domestic complications.

I'd made a promise to Carole and I wanted to stick to it. Never again. No more fighting. Carole was working as a receptionist and, together, we just managed to scrape through.

Truth is, I was terrified of losing her. I'd have crumbled if Carole wasn't around. She remained the single most important thing to ever happen in my life.

Around this time I even ended up employing my old man when I was foreman on a building job in Finborough Road, West London. He didn't like taking orders from me. One time me and a couple of the lads nailed his boots to the floor as a joke. He wasn't happy about that either. Another time we gave him a pie that was so piping hot he dropped it on the floor. I suppose those sort of pranks were my way of letting him know I thought he wasn't much of a dad.

But when the old man found out about the cage fighting he had a right go at me, which at least seemed to prove he cared. 'Are you mad, Son?' he asked.

But then, typical of the old man, he went and asked me if I could get him into one of the fights. No doubt he wanted to gamble a few bob – and I'm not sure he'd have put his money on me, either! Anyway, he never did get in to see me fight and I'm glad about that.

Back in East London my special services continued to be called upon. One of my mum's neighbours was being terrorised by some youths on her estate. This woman had a daughter called Sue who'd been going out with a fella. They'd had a baby and the baby had then died from a hole in the heart, so they were going through a bit of a rough patch. This fella was on drugs, threatened the mother-in-law with a knife and then moved a couple of his mates into the flat. They wouldn't leave and the mother didn't want to involve the cozzers because these fellas were a bit stir crazy. So she asked me to sort out her problem.

I went round to the flat with a pal and knocked on the door. We didn't tell them the real reason why we were there at first but we pretended that one of them had upset me by going round saying bad things on the manor about me. I wasn't going to burst into the flat because then the Old Bill might get involved if a neighbour called them. If it was out on the street I had got half a chance of getting away, whereas if I was inside the flat creating havoc they could corner me and do me. The fellas came steaming out and tried to have a dig at us so we launched ourselves at them. We gave them a right seeing to and warned them that if we saw them around the area we'd kill them.

It worked and they didn't come back to the flat anymore. Sue, the ex-girlfriend then rubbed it in a bit more, telling them I was a psycho and I'd come round and kill 'em if I ever saw them again. I heard they left the manor that day and never returned.

Just a few days later I came to the rescue of yet another local damsel in distress. I was at my mum's house when the front doorbell went and I opened it to find Karen, a teenage friend of Carole's, standing there with a tiny baby in her arms. She was sobbing. 'He's smashing the house up, Carl, please come quick.' Then I noticed the bruising round her cheek-bone and a tiny speck of blood on her upper lip. Say no more.

I waved her into our house and tried to calm her down while finding out exactly what had happened. Then I headed off to her house just round the corner. As I strode up the path, the front door to her maisonette was wide open so I walked straight in.

'Hello. Anyone in?'

'Who the fuck're you?' came a voice out of the darkness.

'I'm Karen's friend.'

'Fuck off.'

Just then, someone loomed out of the pitch black into full view. Then he grabbed a chair and threw it against the wall and started kicking in the telly. I moved in fast.

He next pulled a kitchen knife off a sideboard by the telly and started waving it in my direction. Seeing that knife glinting in the light made me completely lose it. I picked up a chair and hurled it right at him and hit my target. He fell to the ground and I jumped on him. He still had the knife in his right hand.

I sat on his chest with one hand holding his wrist down with the knife still grasped in his palm. Then I began smashing him in the face with my favourite left hook.

'Calm down,' I said with a punch.

'Calm down,' I said with another punch.

'Calm down,' I said with a third punch.

'Get off me. I'll kill ya!' he screamed. Not a good response on his part.

He left me no choice but to then whack him really hard. I caught him at least another half a dozen times with a flurry of punches. On the fifth hit, he went out like a light. I dragged him out of the house by his hair. Then he started coming round.

Meanwhile Carole and Karen had appeared on the pathway. 'Don't kill him, Carl. Please don't kill him,' pleaded Karen.

'He'll live.'

Then I told Carole to go home while Karen waited with me.

I hauled this prat to his feet and dragged him back into the maisonette where I sat him down on one of the few remaining chairs.

'How did all this start?' I asked him.

'She nicked my money.'

By now Karen was in floods of tears and so was her baby: it was bedlam. And then he started yelling again.

'Stop shoutin'!' I ordered. He went quiet.

Then I asked Karen if she still wanted to stay in the flat.

'I love him.'

'What? Even though he's just hit you?' I asked.

Then he chipped in: 'She nicked my money and she deserved a slap.'

'Shut it,' I barked.

'But she nicked my money ...'

'You don't hit a woman for any reason,' I growled, thinking back to my own experiences with my dad and that bastard Terry.

'If I hear you've done this ever again, I'll be back to sort you out.'

I heard that the day after my visit to their flat he found the money he thought she'd nicked down the back of an armchair. I even popped round and helped repair their front door. But I did that for Karen, not him.

Amazingly, they did sort themselves out and they're still together to this day. Sometimes I bump into that bloke in my local and he always tries to buy me a bevy, but I've never accepted one because I don't drink with wife-beaters.

\* \* \*

In the midst of all this, Uncle Pete, who was now based back in England, helped me get some work doing security for the

Rolling Stones, for their UK-based tours. I was even offered the chance of touring with the Stones in Japan but I didn't want to be apart from Carole for three months so I turned that down. At all big UK concerts, there's a pit area between the rock stars and the audience. I was one of the security men responsible for stopping the fans getting on the stage. Naturally, there were lots of birds after the Stones. They'd be constantly asking for backstage passes and some even offered their bodies for it – ridiculous, ain't it?

When the Stones came on, the noise was always out of this world, beyond deafening. Whole mobs of women tried to climb the barriers and we had to grab 'em and then throw 'em out of the arena. There were fights galore and I got lots of scratches but I never used my brute strength on a female. One time I had a tear-up with another minder because he knocked out some poor lady. It was out of order and he had to be taught a lesson.

Uncle Pete also once got me work at a David Bowie concert. There, we got virtually drowned in women's panties – there were so many, we had to kick them out of the way. The smell of pot was also lethal and I've no doubt many of those women were off their heads on something a lot stronger as well. I even came across a few nutty blokes who were I suppose what you'd call gay stalkers. Other women would stuff notes into my pocket, which they wanted me to pass to Bowie. Some of the things they promised in the letters would make your hair stand on end!

I also did the security at two hotel parties after Stones concerts. My main job was to keep journos out. One time these two really gorgeous-looking girls tried to soften me up but I knew what they were up to and told them to take a hike.

Probably the heaviest minding job I ever had was to protect a NatWest Bank executive whose family had been threatened with kidnapping. They lived in Southwark and I had to stick by them virtually every minute of the day and night. Luckily no one ever made a grab for them.

The strangest job assignment I ever had was when I escorted this Russian Mafia type around London. He never once said a word to me over the space of five days. He'd just hand me a piece of paper with an address and off we'd go in the rented limo. A lot of his meetings were in Holiday Inns around London. One time I even had to drive him into one of the roughest parts of the East End and I was amazed because the British crims he met turned out to speak Russian! Later on at that meeting it all got very heated and a couple of shooters were pulled out on the Russian, who then hotfooted it back to the car before we headed straight to Heathrow. I never saw him again but I heard later he copped a couple of bullets on the streets of Moscow.

Around this time my baby sister Lee – by now in her late twenties and the divorced mum of one child – had a big problem with some drug dealers down at a pub she ran in Rochester, Kent. So me and my brother Ian popped over the Dartford Bridge to give her a helping hand. Scum like drug dealers deserve everything they get.

We hung about in the pub one night and picked off five of these pieces of vermin and told them to stay away – permanently. They didn't look too happy but they did what they were told. I decided that me and Ian should stay over at Lee's flat above the pub that night because I had an inkling there might be some follow-up aggro.

Lo and behold, at dawn the following morning, three of these bastards turned up at the pub with baseball bats. Ian and I smacked 'em about a bit and then took their bats off them and gave them a right hiding. They never came back. Sometimes you have to resort to such measures, and no one can tell me they care about a bunch of low-life drug dealers.

Back in Forest Gate, it wasn't just domestics and drug dens that required my personal attention. One time I heard that a sick paedophile bastard had just got out of jail after serving a five-stretch for sexually assaulting kids on my manor. The piece of scum then went back to his old home, just around the corner from where one of his victims still lived. Imagine it. Every day you walk out of your home and come face to face with the vermin that ruined your childhood. Doesn't bear thinking about, does it? Well, as you can no doubt imagine; there was a lot of bad feeling when this sicko got out of clink and started showing his face on the manor once again.

Within a week of him turning up again, he was found shot dead – right between the eyes. What a crying shame! What a pity! If ever anyone had it coming to them, it was this sick piece of dog shit. Everyone on the manor was happy as pie. Even the Old Bill didn't seem too bothered.

Well, that's how it seemed until me and my brother Ian got pulled in by the law for questioning. They wanted to know our movements on the day of the murder because some neighbour had given a description of a heavy-set man wearing a baseball cap being seen outside the victim's house just after he had bought it, so to speak: The cozzers reckoned it was me.

They kept us in for seven hours that day, on the basis of a

description that could have fitted about half a million blokes across East London. It was well out of order but I presumed the law was simply going through the motions. That evening we were let out of the nick and I thought that was the end of it.

But two days later they hauled us in again. They claimed some wrong 'un had put my name in the frame. I suppose it's also possible I got pulled because I was known on the manor as someone who helped others out if they'd got a problem. I would have happily pulled the trigger on a piece of crap like him, but as I said to the Old Bill at the time: 'If I could have shot him I would have. But shooters are not my style.'

The cops were quite decent to me and they made it clear they felt obliged to investigate the murder, but they thought that piece of scum got exactly what he deserved. Eventually the cozzers left us both in peace. Recently I found out who put me in the frame and they know it's not all yet forgotten. I'll pick my moment to confront him.

In 1994 me and Carole could finally afford to move back into our flat in Stratford. Carole let me get a doorman's job in the West End in addition to my day job in the building trade because we needed the money if we were going to start a family. She wasn't too happy, but she knew it was the only way we could get ahead of the game, financially speaking.

Then, out of the blue, my old man reappeared on the scene like the bad penny he always was. Better late than never, I guess. One Saturday, me and him went to see a semi-pro boxing tournament at Walthamstow Town Hall. And who do we bump straight into but Bill and Kenny? My heart sank when I spotted them, and I tried to duck out of sight, but a few minutes later I got a tap on the shoulder and they were soon chatting away as if we were long-lost mates.

I clearly meant so little to them on a personal level that they didn't even ask me if I'd recovered from that last vicious beating in Vegas. They made it clear they'd moved on to a bunch of new fighters but insisted there was still a place for me if I wanted what Bill still called a 'job'.

As we talked, I found myself sweating profusely. I just didn't like being in their company, so I said I had to go because I was with my dad and I didn't want them to meet him. Bill gave one of his shallowest smiles and handed me a business card. 'Kenny and I are now full-time partners. Gissa call some time.'

I was still strapped for cash but just looking at the greasy, money-grabbing expressions on both their faces kept me from feeling tempted. I took the card to be polite before turning and walking away from them. I'd given Carole a solemn promise and I fully intended to stick to it. On the way home, however, that card started burning a hole in my pocket, just like before. I wanted Carole to feel financially secure so that she'd feel happy starting a family. This was a chance to get ahead of the game.

Back home with Carole that night, I tried to bring the subject around to fighting. But the very mention of it turned her into a fury. 'Don't even mention it! You are never going back into that game,' she said. I dropped the matter on the spot. No point in winding her up; better just to leave things alone.

Before I got into bed a few minutes later, I found Bill's card in my top pocket. I took it out, looked at it for a moment and then tore it into shreds. I'd made a commitment and I wasn't going back on my word.

A couple of days later, Carole was out seeing her mum when I got home from a building site, knackered and too hard-up to even pop down my local for a pint. I pulled open the drawer of the kitchen table to see if there was enough change to cover the cost of a packet of fish and chips when I noticed the scraps of Bill's business card, which I'd dropped into the drawer.

I sat at the kitchen table and started putting the pieces of the card together like a tiny jigsaw. At first it was a game, just to see if all the pieces fitted. Then I realised I was succumbing to temptation.

With the entire card reconstructed, I sat and looked down at it, hoping that Carole would walk in and break the spell. But she didn't appear and, like a drug addict looking at a syringe or an alcoholic staring at a bottle of vodka, I finally gave in and called Bill.

I still hated him and Kenny. In fact I hated them even more for tempting me back into the cage. But I needed their money and that was what they relied on. Bill answered the phone after a couple of rings. I told him I was up for fighting in the cage again, but I didn't want to do any ducking and diving like before. I also didn't want to travel. Any fights had to be nearby. I knew that was the only way I could make sure Carole didn't suss I was back in the fight game.

Bill fixed me up with three fights in fast succession. I breezed through them all without getting much more than a few scratches, but the money wasn't as good as before. Two grand was about average and that didn't make much of a dent on our debts. And, of course, the less money, the more fights I had to do in order to earn any decent wedge. They had me by the short and curlies.

But I did notice another big difference about these fights compared to when I'd started out; the crowds were much younger. A lot of them were now drug dealer types. There were also quite a few Essex boys, City traders and even a few posh-speaking stockbroker types. The cage seemed to be widening its appeal. Now it wasn't just hardened crims putting huge bets on their boys. Maybe that was why the prize-money had gone down? Yet Britain was booming at the time. House prices were soaring and people were out enjoying themselves every night of the week. That made my drop in pay even harder to swallow.

Luckily, the soft nature of my opponents meant I suffered very few injuries so I managed to prevent Carole discovering what I was up to. If she knew she'd have given me the order of the boot and I couldn't risk that. Nothing was worth it.

Those three fights helped me completely regain my confidence, even though they didn't exactly stretch me to the limit. I'd learned my lesson in Vegas and I was always very well prepared for each bout. I'd also rediscovered my aggression with a vengeance. To be honest about it, I was really enjoying myself. I loved steamrollering opponents in seconds. It made me feel invincible again. I even started acting like a showman – a bit like my idol Ali. I lapped up the crowd as they stood and cheered me on.

I was determined never to repeat the fuck-ups of the past. I even maintained a different type of fitness from before. I deliberately bulked down so I wasn't as heavy as before which gave me more speed in the cage. And that speed of movement and punches was proving devastating for my opponents.

Naturally, Bill and Kenny were in attendance at every fight, rubbing their hands with glee at the tens of thousands of quid they were no doubt earning by betting on me. They regularly tried to lure me with bigger purses to fight in places like France and Ireland but I turned them down flat.

Carole was pregnant by this time so at least I could save a few bob for fatherhood in the process. But there were a few close shaves with her. She'd noticed the extra money I kept bunging at her. I wasn't slapping down thousands on the dinner table because that was too obvious, but I kept offering to pay for everything. I kept the bulk of the cash hidden, but she'd check my wallet and find more than just a few bob. I got regularly grilled, so I hid some of the cash in my mum's garage. I'd pop round there every so often and make out I was picking up or dropping off tools I'd used on building sites.

My cover story to Carole was that I was working doors in the West End at weekends. But living a secret life in order to avoid hurting the ones I loved proved an even bigger strain than before. I didn't even dare tell Carole when I was training. Instead, I said I was out boozing with the boys. But I believed I was lying for a good cause: the future of my family. More and more frequently, I'd catch Carole looking at me in a strange kind of way, as if she knew exactly what I was up to. Women have an antenna for such things but, for the moment, this seemed the least hurtful way of dealing with the cage.

On 16 May 1995 our baby daughter Melanie was born. It was a twenty-two-hour birth. Carole lost a lot of blood and, in the end, they had to use forceps to pull the baby out into this big, bad world. Poor little Carole and poor little Melanie – it was a close call that shook me to the core.

Rocking tiny Melanie and looking down at an exhausted

Carole, I decided later that same day that I had to walk away from the fight game for good. This was it -the big decision. I'd continue keeping fit and trim – but that was just for the sake of my own health. How could I let those two girls down after what they'd been through?

Even my wayward old man turned up in the hospital to see his granddaughter. He didn't ask me much about what I was up to, but I suppose it's the thought that counts. He did, however, fire me a warning shot about keeping clear of the illegal fight game. No doubt he'd heard something on the grapevine. Then he went and disappeared again, which didn't really bother me because my only priority at the time was Carole and Melanie.

Despite the extra fight money, finances were still tight and Carole had to go back to work as a secretary at Railtrack a couple of months after Melanie's birth. That got to me because I wanted her to be at home looking after the baby. I convinced myself that Carole's working had caused all those problems with the birth.

Then Carole made me promise to give up the door work and I realised that was why she'd gone back to work. It was a testing time for both of us. But we settled into a quiet life of domestic bliss and I began sleeping easily at night for the first time in years. No more red-raw knuckles and aching bones. Money remained tight, but at least me and my family were in one piece.

It's important to point out here that, although we've had some really noisy rows, I'd never lay a finger on my family – it's just not my style and I suppose a lot of it is down to the way my mum brought us up. Men are different. They're all fair game in a way, as I'll always remember what I saw my dad and that arsehole Terry get up to. Carole and I are up and down like yo-

yos really, but I couldn't survive without her. She's in charge of all the money I earn. She doesn't like to spend money unless it's really necessary and she certainly doesn't spend much on herself. When I've been a right pain, I get her flowers and when I've got some cash burning a hole in my pocket, I love buying her jewellery and stuff. I still feel that the best day of my life was the day that I met Carole.

Eighteen months after Melanie's birth, I went out for a rare pint at a pub called the Two Puddings, in Stratford, with a couple of mates. I bumped straight into Kenny and Bill. The grim reapers of the fight game were leaning against the bar, smirking as if they owned the place. Their eyes lit up like a couple of Soho pimps when they spotted me.

'Long time no see,' said Kenny in that soft, charming Irish voice of his. 'Why haven't you belled us?'

'I've gotta kid. I'm gettin' my life on track,' I replied in a matter-of-fact voice, hoping they'd get the message and fuck off.

'Pricey business, being a dad, ain't it?' said Bill.

I ignored him, knowing full well what he was up to.

'We could put a few bob your way,' chipped in Kenny.

'I don't wanna know,' I muttered.

Kenny whipped out a business card and shoved it in my top pocket.

'Call me.'

I didn't reply.

CHAPTER TWENTY

# Tell No One

Not long after bumping into Kenny and Bill, I ran into my old minders Neville and Wayne. They told me that one of Kenny and Bill's fighters had died a couple of weeks back after losing in Ireland. My blood froze as my mind snapped back to what happened to that poor bastard roasted alive after my last visit to Ireland.

'You're better off out of it,' said Wayne. I nodded. Hearing about another fighter's death reconfirmed to me that Kenny and Bill didn't give a toss about 'their boys', as they liked to call us. They'd probably bet on his opponent anyway, I thought to myself. One death wasn't going to get in the way of a good earner for those two slimy rats.

'Keep away from them, bruv,' warned Neville, who had this habit of reading my mind. Wayne and Neville were decent fellas and I appreciated their honesty. I left them that evening even more convinced that any return to the cage would be sheer madness.

Back at home, money was so tight that we had to cancel a holiday in Spain. Carole and I even talked about having a crack at living and working in LA because my big brother John was always saying it was much cheaper to live out there. It was tempting but I convinced Carole that, for the moment, we should battle on because I knew it was easier to avoid certain other issues if we stayed put in East London.

Then fate stepped in when John called up a few weeks later and asked me if I'd be the godfather to his newly born baby son, Alfie. 'Why don't we go out there and take a look at the work situation? Have a break and kill two birds with one stone?' Carole asked me hopefully. She'd had enough of her job and desperately missed Melanie while she worked as a wage slave.

I looked at her in a doubtful sort of way. I had to resist it. I was afraid of what might happen if we went to LA.

'But what if I don't get any work? Then we'll be even worse off when we come back here,' I pointed out.

'It'll do us both good, Carl,' Carole said, giving me a hug and a kiss as we discussed it in front of the telly.

'Let's decide in a day or two,' I said.

I scratched my head nervously and wondered what I was letting myself in for. I didn't want to move to LA but if we went out there then I could earn a big payout and we could come back home and start again.

The next morning I called Kenny from a building site. I'd decided to go for broke. One last fight would set us up for life. 'But this one has to be really worth it, Kenny,' I said.

'Naturally.'

'No, I mean *really* worth it.'

'What? '

That's when I told Kenny I wanted a rematch with the Mexican who'd beaten me in Vegas. That defeat had been niggling away at me for years. Kenny said he would see what he could do, 'but I can't make any promises, son.' Yeah right, I thought to myself.

I met Kenny and Bill the following evening in a pub in Stratford. They were well suspicious of my reasons for wanting the rematch.

'Why now?' asked Bill.

'I want that Mexican back. I'm owed a rematch if he's still fightin".'

'I'm not sure we can do it, son,' said Kenny, examining me through increasingly narrowing eyes as if I was up to no good.

A few minutes later they got up and left the pub promising to 'be in touch'. They didn't seem too happy to have me back in the fold.

About a week later, Kenny belled me on my mobile.

'The man you're after is still fighting. D'you want me to set it up?'

I told Kenny I planned to visit my brother John in LA and that I wanted the fight to happen within forty-eight hours of my nephew's christening in Santa Monica.

'I'll call you back,' said Kenny. The match seemed to hold as much appeal for him as a lump of old rice pudding. He didn't like me calling the shots, but on the other hand he couldn't resist the dollar signs clicking up in front of his eyes.

A couple of days later we had a meeting in the Railway

Tavern, in Forest Gate. Bill and Kenny looked even more flash than before. They had two meaty minders in tow, who I insisted sat on a table at the other side of the saloon bar while we got down to business.

First off, they offered me £22,000. I knew they had more cash to spare so I countered that with a demand for £10,000 more. They looked well pissed off, especially since I'd got them to organise the fight before we'd agreed the money. But this fight was to be my parting shot and I wanted enough dough for me and Carole to buy our own house in London – otherwise it wasn't worth it. Knowing that made me a tough negotiator. A few years earlier, I'd have backed down rather than risk losing the fight, but now I didn't give a flying fuck. It was all or nothing.

Kenny and Bill sussed I was deadly serious and it bothered them big time. I must have seemed like a different person from before. They'd been used to this lump of meat who just did what he was told while they scammed five figures out of each one of my victories. They also didn't appreciate that this fight was motivated by a revenge factor.

Kenny and Bill carried on haggling with me about money. 'Twenty-two grand is a generous deal,' said Bill.

'Well then, forget it,' I replied, knowing full well they'd be dead men walking if they tried to pull out of the fight.

They looked at each other nervously – and a bit confused. I bet none of their fighters ever gave them this much grief. I was making demands. I could tell from their faces they thought I was taking the piss.

I took a sip on my third pint of lager, lit up yet another fag and sat there in total silence. That's when I caught Kenny eyeing me with a slight nod of the head and realised they thought I was going to be a lamb to the slaughter. It was exactly what I wanted them to think.

I coughed heavily.

'You keepin' fit then?' asked Kenny.

'Course,' I replied, while still coughing my guts up. Kenny laughed a bit nervously.

'You sure you're up for it?'

I shot up and looked down at him.

'You takin' the piss?'

'Only askin',' said Kenny, backing down with a false grin on his face.

Bill, to his credit, said nothing but the look of contempt on his face told me everything I needed to know.

Still standing, I announced: 'Meeting adjourned, gentlemen. Call me when you've got what I want.'

Kenny leaned over to shake my hand but I ignored him and walked to the bar where a couple of old mates were supping their pints. Then Kenny came up to me and whispered in my ear: 'Thirty-two grand for a win.' He left the pub before I'd had time for it all to sink in. I'd pulled it off. Even if I did cop it in the cage, the loser's prize was bound to be enough for Carole and the baby to be properly looked after.

Back at home, Carole looked very unconvinced when I told her I'd just got a new job as a doorman and wouldn't be around most evenings. At least this time I wouldn't be bulking up like before so she wouldn't spot any change in my shape. But that antenna of Carole's immediately picked up on what I was saying.

'You sure it's just a doorman's job?' she asked, her eyes narrowing.

'Yeah, of course,' I replied, knowing full well it was better to make my lies brief and to the point.

'I'm off if you're havin' me on,' warned Carole, and I knew she meant it.

I still insisted it was just a doorman's job. She looked daggers at me.

'That's it then, I'm going,' she screamed. 'I hope she's worth it.'

She stormed into the bedroom and began packing her bags. Once again, my misses thought I was knocking off another woman when all I was trying to do was earn enough money to buy the house of our dreams.

'Don't be daft, babe,' I said, but of course I didn't sound very convincing because I was lying.

I had to tell her the truth before it was too late.

'It's not another bird. It's a fight,' I blurted it out at high speed.

Carole stopped in her tracks. 'What?'

'I've got a big fight lined up. It'll give us enough dough to buy ourselves a proper house here, Carole. We won't need to live in LA. I'm doin' it for us.' I lied and told her Bill and Kenny had agreed a £32,000 fee 'win or lose'. Truth is, I didn't know what loot she'd get if I flopped.

'That money'll bail us out of here, babe,' I said, pleading. 'Just a few minutes' work and we're made for life.'

'Yeah, and I'll end up a widow with a little child. Great.'

'I won't lose, babe. No way. Look at me. I've never been fitter in my life. This is the big one. This is the one that'll put us on a different level. You've gotta believe me.'

Carole didn't answer this time but at least she put her bag down. I'd won a narrow victory, but I knew I'd pushed Carole to the edge and I couldn't do it ever again.

Strong women like Carole don't forget things in a hurry. She might have backed down about leaving, but she was still annoyed and very worried about my safety.

In April 1997 we boarded a plane to LA but Carole still wasn't really talking to me. At least she'd come with me which meant we'd get through this together. Within a few hours of touching down at LAX, I was on the blower to Kenny at his apartment in Venice Beach. Bill was staying at his place.

'Still on for £32,000?' I asked.

'Yep,' he muttered through gritted teeth. I was enjoying every minute of it. I felt as if I was in complete control for the first time in my career in the cage. I found out that I'd only get half that amount if I lost, and decided to own up to Carole.

'But I'm not going to lose, babe,' I said giving her a hug. She didn't seem too convinced.

Neither was Kenny. He and Bill had their doubts but I knew they wouldn't try to put me off because there was too much money at stake. I wanted them to put all their money on the other man, convinced I'd lose. Neither of them had even asked me if I was training hard. They didn't give a toss whether I won or lost.

The following day, me, Carole and little Melanie went to Disneyland. I loved it and so did Melanie. But I could tell from the serious expression on Carole's face that she was very worried about me. Even at the christening of John's baby son Alfie there was a lot of tension between us.

'So when's it happening?' she whispered to me as we walked out of the church.

'Anytime now.'

'Great ...' said Carole in a sarcastic tone of voice.

I called up Kenny a couple of hours later to ask when the fight was.

'Day after tomorrow, at that same place in Vegas,' muttered Kenny.

That evening, back at John's apartment in Santa Monica I told him I didn't want him to come with me this time. 'I need you to stay at home with Michelle and Carole and keep an eye on them just in case anything goes pear-shaped,' I said.

'What d'you mean?' asked John.

'Don't worry about it, big bruv. just trust me. It's better this way.'

'But you gotta have someone with you. Someone you can trust.'

'They've got a couple of British minders who live here coming with me. It'll be fine.'

How I wished Neville and Wayne were going to be alongside me in Vegas. But we were a long way from East London. That evening, John and I went running near Santa Monica Pier. He pushed me as hard as he could because he knew that my fitness was crucial to my success.

As we ran back through the streets of Santa Monica I looked at the deep orange glow of the sun as it dipped slowly into the Pacific Ocean and wondered if I'd just got myself in too deep. When I got back to the apartment a few minutes later, Carole looked worried and exhausted. What the hell was I doing putting her through this all over again? But then I thought of

Kenny and Bill and the smell of revenge wafted through my nostrils. It had to be worth it ...

## CHAPTER TWENTY-ONE

# **Return Flight**

I'd been thinking about this moment for months and months, before I'd even set up the Vegas rematch. Every time I laid a brick on a building site and it cracked in two I felt that was what I'd like to do to Bill and Kenny: smack 'em together until they cracked into tiny pieces because they'd never really given a fuck about me. They'd used and abused me for years. But for the moment I'd bite my tongue and play dumb for a windfall that I hoped would set me and my family up for life.

Bill and Kenny picked me up in Santa Monica with their two English minders in a black stretch limo to take me to the airport for the Vegas flight. Their flash motor was yet more evidence of the money they'd earned out of me. But this time I'd nailed them down for the purse and that had got right up their hooters.

I could feel their irritation even as we rode in that limo to

LAX. No doubt they thought they couldn't lose, whatever the outcome of the fight. I could see in their eyes they thought I was nothing more than a stupid lump of lard.

'You fit then?' said Kenny, before giving Bill a big wink.

Fucking arsehole thought I hadn't spotted it. They were really getting on my tits. They no doubt thought I was walking into a thrashing. Maybe they were right, but I had a secret game plan and I was sticking to it.

I didn't respond.

Then Kenny asked me again if I was fit and healthy. I'd been very careful not to wear tight-fitting clothes so they couldn't make out whether I was in shape or not. I ignored them again and asked for a drink instead – something I'd never done before a fight in my life. Kenny pulled open the minibar in between the soft white leather limo seats and poured me a huge bourbon. I knocked it back in one gulp. They looked at each other, then back to me.

'You want another one?'

'Why not?' I replied, lighting a fourth Marlboro Light. They were loving every moment, but I didn't give a toss that they thought I was a fat lump about to get a thrashing. By the time we got to LAX they were treating me as if I was not only stupid but also a drunk. Truth was, the adrenaline was rushing so fast through my body that the alcohol had little or no effect on me. I was buzzing with anticipation, and had Bill and Kenny in my sights.

'You sure you can handle this one?' asked Kenny, just before we clambered out of the limo.

'Yeah!' I drooled.

Just then Bill chipped in merrily: 'There's no turning back now, Son.'

'Turnin' back?' I grabbed him by the lapels drunkenly. 'I'm gonna kill that bastard.'

I slurped the bourbon out of the bottom of my glass and slammed it down on the armrest. Bill was smirking at Kenny again. It was a look of sheer contempt that they yet again thought I hadn't noticed.

They stuck me on an aisle seat next to the two English minders on the plane out to Vegas. These two meat merchants barely said a word, but they seemed happy to order me another bourbon. Just before we landed, one of them perked up and asked me: 'How you feelin' then?'

'Mind your own fuckin' business,' I snapped back.

It wasn't difficult sounding aggressive, because I meant every word of it. This bout was going to be different from all the rest. Despite the booze and the fags I felt on top of the fucking world. Mentally and physically I believed I was numero uno. But you can never be sure if you're kidding yourself in this game.

There was another rented stretch limo waiting for us at Las Vegas Airport. We headed down the main strip past the biggest casinos and then turned into a vast open-air car park behind the big hall that was the fight venue. My pre-match diet of bourbon and Marlboro Lights had continued to amuse Kenny and Bill on the trip from the airport.

I realised the moment I walked into the hall that this bout really had been hyped as the Big One. There were many more people than the last Vegas clash. The expectant buzz was there for all to see and feel.

'This the only fight on the bill?' I asked Kenny.

'They're all here for you, Son,' he replied, but I could tell from the tone of his voice he didn't mean a word of it.

I told Kenny and Bill to make sure I wasn't referred to as the 'English Bulldog' or 'London Limey' this time. I hated those nicknames and I also wanted to remain as anonymous as possible. I preferred everyone to think I was just a desperate nobody, out for drunken revenge on a tasty local fighter who'd given me a thrashing a few years back and was about to do it again.

I stopped about thirty feet from the cage, blinked and cleared my throat. That's when I wobbled a bit on my pins.

'You alright, Son?' asked Bill.

I nodded and carried on heading towards the cage, wearing the usual jeans, but with an old baggy sweatshirt over my T-shirt.

Kenny and Bill veered away from me and my two minders to speak with a smartly dressed fella in a light brown double-breasted suit. I couldn't hear what they were saying but it was obviously important. Then they handed over a huge wedge of cash. It must have been tens of thousands of dollars. They were placing their bets but I knew it wasn't on me. After all, I'd lost the last fight and now I looked like shit. Bets were probably in the region of three to one against me at the very least.

I made a point of not taking off that old sweatshirt until I was just about to get in the cage because I didn't want anyone – especially Bill and Kenny – to see what condition I was in.

The crowd got more and more noisy as I approached. The compère was already standing in the cage with a mike in his hand. 'Ladies and gentlemen, this is the fight of the year. It's a rematch. We've got Paco from Mexico City against the mystery man.'

'Who da fuck is he?' screamed one voice from the audience.

'He got whipped a couple of years back. Now he's back for more.'

'Yeah, he looks real fat,' yelled another above the din.

As I got even closer to the cage I noticed a lot people holding bottles of champagne by the neck. Others were snorting cocaine off their clenched fists. Bill and Kenny stopped just in front of me to hand another bookie some more cash. I was well chuffed because I hoped they were about to lose a fortune.

I then went through a drunken warm-up routine. Much louder and more obvious than ever before – I suppose some would call it showboating. The crowd laughed as if I was some kind of idiot. I even did a defiant one-minute Ali shuffle but they kept yelling at me like I was a stand-up comic telling lousy jokes. Across the other side of the cage my opponent looked totally chilled and super-confident. He was smiling and waving to the crowd. They loved him. I was just the patsy about to get a serious beating.

Then I racked up the tension by stabbing my finger in the air at him.

'I'm goin' to 'ave you,' I screamed. 'I'm goin' to tear you to pieces!'

I just couldn't help myself. The crowd were loving it for all the wrong reasons.

I looked across at Bill, pulled my cheeks up with my thumbs and forefingers to make a jokey, smiley face. He didn't smile back. He was looking at me as if I was some sort of crazy, drunken lunatic.

Dramatic classical music played over the PA system, making the atmosphere even more awesome. In earlier years, I might have felt intimidated, but not today. I was on top of the fucking world. The buzz was tingling through every bone in my body. And the crowd's attitude didn't bother me one bit.

Just then the compère coughed to clear his mike. 'Are the fighters ready to fight?'

We both nodded at each other.

'Will the warriors please enter the cage.'

*Warriors*? Typical Yanks – they have to give everything a slab of top spin.

Just before I stooped to get through the doorway to the cage, I ripped off the old baggy sweatshirt I'd been wearing. That's when I spotted Kenny's eyes examining my physique. His expression now wasn't the chirpy, smiling one I'd grown to hate. He nudged Bill and whispered something in his ear. 'I'll show 'em,' I thought to myself. 'I'll fuckin' show 'em.'

I entered the cage, crouching down low to squeeze through the doorway. This time I wouldn't be making the same mistake as before. I sprang up into the cage and landed on both feet, steady as a rock. Then I held back patiently. I sized up my opponent then beckoned him towards me.

'Come on, pretty boy. Come and get me,' I yelled at him. 'Here boy, here boy, heeere boy.'

He didn't budge. He wanted me to go to him. To steam in blindly like I'd done at the opening of our last bout.

'Come to me, gringo,' he screamed. His eyes bored holes in me from twenty feet away.

*'Tu puto madre.'*

That means 'motherfucker' and, as you know, no-one insults my mum and gets away with it.

But then I surprised him by squatting down and resting my

fists on the wooden floor for balance. He looked confused. I put up one hand and started beckoning him with my finger again. The crowd were confused and went completely quiet.

'Kill the crazy British motherfucker,' said one voice.

'Go get him!'

Finally my flashy opponent fell for the bait and started heading for me. I stayed in that squatting position until he got really close. Then I jumped up and threw a punch right under him. The sheer force of my body movement guaranteed it was a sledgehammer.

He wobbled, almost lost his footing and crashed past me right into the mesh. He quickly tried to turn and swing at me but completely missed. I was as steady as a rock and then started moving around him Ali-style as he leaned against the mesh trying to recover his composure. His face was black with fury, but there was an air of confusion about him, too. Then he came at me, wildly throwing punches into thin air. I caught him in the neck with a sharp snap which just missed his Adam's apple, followed by a swift left that smashed into his cheek with an almighty crack. He pulled back away from me to give himself a moment to reform.

'Come on, little girl. Come to daddy,' I goaded with a sly smile, beckoning him with my finger yet again. 'Come to daddy.' I'd insulted his macho pride and he couldn't handle it. That's when he totally lost it and came charging back towards me. I was on top, no doubt about it. I caught him with a flurry of uppercuts to the face and forehead: bang, bang, bang. He reeled backwards before he could even throw a punch. The crowd still didn't get it. But then they did have a lot of dough riding on my opponent.

'Kill him!'

'Put that asshole outta his misery.'

The shouts from the crowd encouraged a red mist to descend in front of my eyes. I was on a roll of vengeance but it wasn't really this fighter I was after. I paused for a moment and he caught me with a decent right-hander to my face. I jerked back in response. He then got me with a strong flurry of stinging punches. They were good-quality stabs that wiped out my surge of confidence.

I knew I had to become even stronger. How dare he try to get back into the fight? I had to make him pay. So I moved in for a full-scale attack, headbutting him twice and then hitting him with a flurry of punches to his body. He legs were buckling so I pulled him towards me and caught him with a steamroller left to the back of his neck. At least two more bone-crunching headbutts followed in quick succession. Then I caught him with both fists, one after the other, snap, snap. He fell backwards and crashed low against the wire mesh wall of the cage. Then I laid in with a high left-sided kick to the head. My blind rage was in overdrive. I was like a runaway tank, ripping up all in my path. Some people in the audience were screaming for me to stop but I didn't care.

Then my opponent began struggling to his feet once again. Seeing him wobbling on his pins helped me regain some composure and, blinking, I felt my sanity return. I caught him with two huge sledgehammer knocks to the body and face. His legs shook like jelly again and he crashed to the floor. I looked across at Bill and Kenny and grinned, exposing my black gumshield. They looked far from happy.

Truth is I had no real truck with this other fighter. I wanted to teach those two greedy bastards the biggest lesson of their scumbag lives. My primary aim had always been to hit Bill and Kenny where it would hurt them most – in their wallets.

With my opponent half kneeling in front of me, I sent in a flurry of vicious kicks that hit their target with crunching efficiency. He crumpled to the floor. I looked down at him. He was clearly out cold. Then I leaned down and put my hand in his mouth and tried to pull him up by the teeth. He was about as useful as a sack of dead squirrels. So I turned and looked into the crowd. They'd switched sides and were cheering their socks off for me. It was pretty decent considering I'd just cost them a bundle. And it was a magical feeling, I can tell you. I bowed to the audience just as a water bottle was thrown into the cage. It was all over. His team had thrown in the towel.

But I had just one more bit of business to attend to.

The two English minders snapped open the bolt of the door to the cage and I scrambled out. My opponent was still out cold and two men, one of whom looked like a doctor, were leaning over him. I was still buzzing with pent-up energy as I walked through the cheering crowds towards the car park where the limo was waiting. I'd proved myself right and had shown a lot of people they were wrong to take me for a fool.

Bill and Kenny were leaning against the limo with serious expressions on their faces as I arrived. 'Well done,' both of them said quickly at exactly the same time.

'Where's my dough?' I snapped at them, enjoying every minute of their obvious discomfort.

'It's in the motor,' said Kenny, whose ever-present smile had finally been wiped from his face.

I clambered into the stretch with Bill, Kenny and the two English minders. As we drove to the airport you could have heard a pin drop, the silence was so overwhelming.

After a couple of minutes, Kenny handed me an envelope. I looked up and caught Bill's expression. He looked terrible. 'Thanks,' I said. I didn't bother counting the money at the time but it turned out to contain $50,000 – the £32,000 fee I'd been promised, in dollars. Neither Bill nor Kenny said another word on the journey along the Vegas strip, not even when a hooker in a white leather mini-skirt tried to lean into our limo and offer her services at a red light. Then Kenny pulled a bottle of Bourbon out of the minibar between the seats. He poured out three glasses and handed me one. 'No thanks,' I said merrily. 'I hate the stuff.' Kenny looked at Bill, sighed, and at that moment they at last knew they'd been had.

## CHAPTER TWENTY-TWO

# Nil By Mouth

The limo that picked me up at LAX dropped me around the corner from my brother John's apartment in Santa Monica because I didn't want Bill and Kenny knowing exactly where he lived. When I finally rolled into the apartment in the early hours, John was still waiting up for me.

'I did it, John. I fuckin' did it!' I hugged him. He didn't know whether to laugh or cry.

'You should have seen the look on those bastards' faces when they realised they'd been had. It was sweet, mate. Fuckin' sweet.'

John told me that Carole and Michelle had drunk so much to calm their nerves, they'd ended up crashing a couple of hours earlier. I had a bloody nose, a sore mouth and two shiners, so John helped clean me up a bit. We sat there swigging back a few beers and had a good chat about old and new times while I soaked my red-raw knuckles in a bucket of ice.

The sun was coming up before I finally made my way towards the bedroom. Carole was fast asleep, with baby Melanie next to her in the crib. I got into the bed and just lay there staring at Carole for what seemed like hours. I'll never leave you again, I thought to myself. Never.

I woke up later that day at lunchtime to find Carole gently dabbing at my swollen face with an ice-cold flannel. I smiled at her and was about to say how sorry I was when she beat me to it: 'It's good to have you back.'

Then Carole kissed me and added: 'I didn't think you'd be clever enough to pull it off, babes.'

'Is that it?' I asked, expecting a flood of tears and anger over what had happened.

'That's it,' said Carole simply.

I gave her the envelope containing the cash. A couple of days later we set off for London. Before we boarded the plane, John made me promise in front of Carole that I would never fight again. I agreed and we hugged John goodbye. It really was over this time.

We used a lot of that money on a deposit for a decent house rather than the shoebox we'd been living in. I also took two months off in order to rethink our lives. It was a good decision because we sorted out a lot of things in that time.

About five or six months later an invitation turned up in the post for me and Carole to go to a dinner dance. It was from Kenny. Carole didn't want me to go, but I told her I wanted to attend 'just for a laugh'.

She didn't see the joke. 'You'll just go and get yourself into more trouble. What's the point in upsetting those sort of people?'

'I gotta go,' I replied. 'There's no way I'll go back to fighting. I promise. On the baby's life.' And I really did mean it this time.

Neville and Wayne turned out to be at Kenny's dinner dance, held at a function hall in a back street of Ilford. Everyone was wearing dinner jackets except for me, in a black leather bomber jacket. Why should I care? In any case, I didn't plan to stay long. Wayne and Neville laughed when they saw me walk in. They also grinned when I said I'd given up the fight game.

'Bet you still got the bug,' said Wayne.

'No way.'

Just then Bill waved me over to his table. He was with Kenny and a bunch of brassy-looking blondes who couldn't have been their wives.

'How's life?' asked Bill.

'Excellent,' I replied.

'Might have somethin' I could put your way,' said Bill.

'What?' I asked.

'You know what I mean.'

'You don't get it, do you?' I said before turning away from them. 'It's over.'

As I strolled out, Bill and Kenny were looking right at me, no doubt hoping another mug like me might come along one day.

A few months later I called up Bill: He must have thought I'd changed my mind and was coming out of retirement. All I wanted was a video tape of a fight to show the makers of the film *Shiner,* which I was working on as fight adviser. Bill was far from happy. 'No way, Carl,' he responded. 'But if you're after a "job" ...'

'Leave it out, Bill,' I said, putting the receiver down without even bothering to say goodbye. If you live by the sword you eventually die by it, or so they say.

Working on a film was interesting, but it was only short-term and I was soon back in the building game, which, thanks to another property boom, was very busy.

On 22 November 1998, our second daughter Jaime was born. That sealed my decision not to fight 150 per cent. My family really had taken first place from the moment I'd won that bout in Vegas.

I suppose the cage was in many ways a reflection of my life because I often seemed to be trapped, whether it was by Bill and Kenny, or by that bastard who ended my legit boxing career, or by my childhood ruined by Dad doing a runner and that bully Terry making my life a misery.

Just after I quit the game for good, I saw a brilliant film called *Nil By Mouth*, directed and written by actor Gary Oldman, and starring that diamond geezer Ray Winstone. I've never cried so much at a movie because it brought so many unhappy memories pouring back to me. I later heard that the film was based on Oldman's life as a kid in London. It featured the same sort of domestic chaos that dominated my childhood. At least I'd managed to escape the abuse, thanks to Carole, my mum, my kids and my brute strength.

But I'd so nearly lost it all. Everything ended up centring on that last fight. It was the ultimate gamble that could have cost me my life and my family. And now I hoped I would never put them through that ever again.

## CHAPTER TWENTY-THREE

# The Big Easy

For four long years I kept out of bovver and avoided all the old haunts. I really liked the peaceful life at home with Carole and the girls. The nearest I came to a punch up was when some fella cut me up at the traffic lights. It was a good feeling not to be looking over my shoulder all the time and I was desperate to keep it that way for the rest of my life.

The first edition of this book had come out and I'd made a few bob out of it, so life was pretty sweet. But I knew it would never last *that* long.

Then in the winter of 2004/2005 the building game started drying up a bit and I began getting twitchy about how I was going to pull in enough cash to provide for my family. I guess that's the way it goes with most people. You hit a dry patch and you start really stressing out about how you're going to pay the bills and stuff like that. My priority was – and always will be – Carole and the kids.

One day in late spring 2005, I was out on a rare building job over in the East End when I met this fella called Dan who'd I'd known back in my cage fighting days. He'd been quite a tasty scrapper himself as it happens. Dan was a decent fellow. Not flash or outwardly hard but he could certainly pack a mean punch when required. Dan and I had also worked the doors at a couple of nightclubs together so he knew all about me and my dangerous old habits. Anyway, one day he asked me out of the blue if I was still up for a scrap, although he did it in a very clever, roundabout sort of way.

'How's the money situation goin' at the moment, son?'

I knew what he was on about before he'd finished the sentence.

'I'm always on the lookout for a decent earner,' I answered, watching a Cheshire-cat grin come over his face as I talked.

Next thing I know he's saying, 'I know this fella in Dagenham who read yer book and he reckons he could 'ave ya.'

I always wondered how long it'd take for some Big Mouth to get wound up by my book. There's still a lot of so-called hard nuts out there who reckon they could take on the entire SAS and beat 'em.

Then Dan chipped in, 'He's no youngster but he's got a bit of form.'

I shrugged my shoulders.

'So?'

'And he's from Spain,' added Dan, as if I was supposed to be impressed. Dan then explained he'd beaten one of this bloke's cousins in a scrap, which was how he came to meet him in the first place.

Meanwhile, I had only one thing on my mind – the cash. 'You better get a meet sorted, old son.'

I must have been bloody mad. Back home everything was sweet as a nut, apart from being a bit short of a bob or two. What the hell was I doing putting all that at risk? Carole was happy 'cause I'd kept out of trouble. We had a lovely house, two beautiful daughters. I'd even just splashed out a fortune on having the windows done, which might have been why I was a little brasso! But then it's too easy to look for excuses ain't it?

Trouble was, my mate Dan had just put a big cake in front of me and I couldn't resist eating it. I could feel the excitement building up inside me within seconds of him first mentioning the fight.

'So he thinks he's a hard nut does he?' I asked, already enjoying all that hardman banter once again.

I knew there and then I wanted this fight to happen. There's no point in denying it. I was completely up for it. I was well pumped up. There was no holding me back!

So I agreed to meet this Spanish geezer a few days later in a pub in Dagenham called The Magpie. I'd actually helped build an extension to it, which was why I remembered it so well. Those evil old bastard promoters Bill and Kenny would never have allowed me to meet an opponent ahead of a fight. But Dan was a much straighter shooter, if you know what I mean. In any case, by meeting the Spaniard first I knew I could always back out if I didn't like the look of him.

When the day of the meet came around, Dan had wanted us to turn up mob handed but I said what's the point? If he wanted to fight in the pub he'd be bloody stupid. So I had Dan watching from nearby just in case someone jumped up and took a pop at me but I knew nothing would happen. Although I did make

sure Dan was packing just in case the entire meet was some sort
of stunt by one of my old battered opponents trying to get
revenge on me.

I made a point of winding up the Spaniard by turning up 20
minutes late for the meet in that pub. When I finally walked in
and saw him sitting there, I knew immediately he was the man
because he was all bulked up like Arnie S and sitting there
looking really manic all on his own. He even had cuts all over
him, which immediately told me he wasn't much of a fighter.
The Spaniard had short, cropped dark hair with a little razor
line through his scalp. Very pretty.

He also looked like he weighed in at around 18 stone and was
about six foot two, which is an inch or so taller than me. His
neck was so thick he looked more like a weightlifter than a
fighter, which was good news because these sort of pumped up
geezers are always the easiest to put on the floor.

But the best sign of all was the empty plate and a couple of pint
beer glasses in front of him. A real fighter wouldn't be tucking
into a stodge and downing pints for a meeting like this. He spoke
pretty good English although he had quite a broken Spanish
accent. Turned out he was 41, a year older than me. Then I
noticed his big barrel of a gut. I knew I'd have him no trouble.

As I sat across the table from him, he tried to come across as
confident, bolshie and flash. At one stage he even growled, 'I'll
take you on.' Simple as that. But that just made me realise he
was a bit twitchy. Then I grinned at him. Stupid bastard didn't
realise why.

Then it was my turn to chuck in a bit of banter.

'You're not much cop, are ya son?' I said, looking right into
his eyes.

He tried to look daggers back at me then. But I could tell behind his watery, dark brown eyes that he was nervous.

I knew he had a couple of heavies sitting nearby just in case we kicked off there and then but, as I said earlier, that would have been stupid. I wanted the prize money, not the satisfaction of knocking him flying. Having a stand-up in a boozer just because I didn't like the look of a man wouldn't have earned me a penny.

Then the Spaniard growled again.

'I'm gonna have you.'

This was getting silly. I knew he was shitting hot bricks.

'Whatever you say, old son…' I replied, as cool as the proverbial cucumber. 'Now what about the readies?'

That's when he barked back: 'You get four grand loser's purse, winner's twelve.'

Sounded good to me because I knew which purse I'd get.

'Done.'

I put me hand out to shake on it. He grabbed hold of it, which I didn't like one bit.

'So when's the meet?' I asked, snatching my hand away from his.

'We be in touch soon.'

That's when I noticed his whole face had completely changed expression. He was clearly worried that I was so confident. He must have thought I'd haggle with him over the cash.

Then he said in a much softer voice.

'I speak to my people and we agree a date.'

'That's cool.'

All I cared about was giving him a hammering and earning the cash. It hadn't taken much to turn me back into a fighter.

So that was that.

The Spaniard sat there as I got up and left the pub. All I knew was that his promoter would be putting the money up. I didn't care who paid it out as long as it was there to collect immediately after I'd crushed that fat old Spaniard into the ground.

Now I might have looked cool and confident in front of the Spaniard but the enormity of what I'd just done really hit me after I got out of the pub. What the hell was I playing at? Carole would be furious with me for going back on my word. I'd promised her I'd never fight again. But instead of facing up to what I'd just gone and done I went straight home and tried to put the whole thing to the back of my mind. No point in telling her just in case it never happened.

But then other questions started going through my head. Am I going to get out of this alive? What if it's all some kind of trap set up by Kenny and Bill? But then I remembered the Spaniard's nervous face and I knew I could have him easy. I was 100% certain. The bigger they are, the harder they fall.

If that Spaniard had looked wiry and fit as a fiddle like Jean Claude Van Damme at his peak with veins sticking out and muscles to match I would definitely have thought twice about it. But this fella was meat to the slaughter. I had no doubts. But then I couldn't afford to have any, could I?

If I'd thought there was any chance of getting beaten I would have asked for a lot more cash because that loser's money was chickenfeed to me. I'd have wanted more than double that fee just to walk into a fight arena. But I knew that Spaniard was a useless lump. No way was he the real McCoy. He might have been a bit of a hard man, but he moved and talked too slowly to be any real threat. And he never once got up out of his chair for me to take a proper look at him. Seeing that gut on him had been more than enough for me.

I knew I had a maximum of four weeks to sort myself out physically, which is not a lot of time when you've been out of the game for so long. My regular work as a builder was physical, but this was a different kettle of fish altogether. I went down the gym every day and started working on a bag to strengthen up. I hadn't used a bag in years and it took me a week just to get back into the swing of it, but then I started to really enjoy it.

I told Carole I was going to the gym, but I didn't say why. At first she didn't suspect a thing and just thought I was on a health kick. But then she noticed I was also watching my food. I started insisting on mainly white meat and salads and rice and pasta and things like that. No chips. So when I started stuffing back huge bowls of spaghetti it was pretty obvious to Carole that I was up to no good. After all, I'm not really a big eater usually. I like drinking fluids like milk and all those nourishment drinks but when I started asking her to pick up 24 cans of nutridrink at the supermarket she got well suspicious.

A couple of weeks after I'd agreed to the fight, Carole fronted me up one night.

'Wot's goin' on, Carl?' she asked.

'Wot you mean, babes?'

I must have looked a bit shifty when I replied but in my heart of hearts I knew there was no point in lying. So I hesitated and then told her everything. I had to. She hit the roof.

'What the hell are you playin' at?' Carole screamed.

'It'll be easy,' I said, trying desperately to make it all sound very 'normal'.

But Carole was far from convinced.

'I want a divorce,' she screamed at me. 'I'm not gonna let you put me through this again.'

I was absolutely stunned and backed down immediately.

'I'll call it off then,' I said. 'It's only money. It ain't that important. Just money that we desperately need.'

Trying the old emotional blackmail routine was like a red rag to a bull in a chinashop.

'I don't want anything to do with this,' said Carole. 'You told me you'd never fight again and you've lied. I've had it with you.'

I held my hands up.

'Alright. Alright. I won't do it. I promise.'

But I was lying. Carole knew it and so did I. I was hooked in. I could tell immediately from the look on her face she knew I was still going through with it.

We never mentioned it again but Carole made sure I knew how she felt by not talking to me. She was steaming mad with me and I was more scared by that than any scrap in a cage. I didn't want to lose Carole and the girls. Nothing was worth that. But something was driving me on to do this fight. I don't know if it was pride, the money or just a bit of old fashioned recklessness, but I still wanted to do it. What a selfish bastard I was.

And Carole remained deadly serious about getting a divorce. I knew she meant it because of the way she'd completely stopped talking to me. Worse still, I'd come home from work and she wouldn't be there. If she was, she'd glare at me and not say a word. I felt like shit but I never once truly considered backing out of that fight. What the hell was going on in my head? My own beloved wife was looking daggers at me every minute of the day. You could cut the atmosphere in the house with a sledgehammer. She didn't want to know me. I felt completely alone in many ways but maybe that was the way I liked it? Maybe that was the best way to prepare for a fight? I must have been off my rocker.

But all the way through that training period I kept telling myself I needed the money and I wanted to believe I was still a top fighter. The way that Spaniard had come across in the boozer that day had narked me. I didn't like his attitude one bit. He thought he could take me easy and I wasn't having any of that. No way. I'll take you out. No trouble, I thought to myself. Fuck knows if I was right.

About a week before the fight, I met up with Dan again and he'd spoken to the promoter who said everything was now laid on. We decided to get a couple of minders to come along to the fight just in case there were any problems. After all, we had no guarantee we'd get the cash right afterwards so these heavies would make sure I got what was rightfully mine – my winner's fee.

I had the feeling this scrap would be much more out in the open than all those other fights I'd had across the globe. The same basic anything-goes rules applied. But the build-up didn't seem so shady. Those old promoters Kenny and Bill had definitely kept it all so cloak and dagger to stop me getting too involved. Those two old bastards didn't want to tell me what they were earning and that was also why they always sprung it on me at the last minute. Dan and this new bunch were much more up front.

Dan told me during that meet in the pub that the location would be my old stomping ground of Dagenham, not far from those docks where I'd once got such a bad pasting.

Dan said he didn't know much more about the Spaniard but he was still very confident I'd have him. I intended to give Dan £2,000 out of my purse if I won.

The day before the fight I plucked up the courage to tell Carole about the details of the fight and that it was scheduled to happen at eight the following evening.

'It's tomorrow, babes.'

'I don't care,' was her only response. But I felt that by telling her at least I'd been honest about it all.

That day of the fight I trained hard. I started with a run for half a mile, then a bit of bag work down the gym. Back home I ate well and gulped down a lot of water.

I knew the key to my success was in my head not body. I needed to take myself down a tunnel of concentration so that by the time I took a crack at that Spaniard I'd be virtually invincible.

But Carole was still not talking to me.

So I got up, walked towards the hall of the house and said I'd be back in two hours. That was a pretty stupid thing to say since I might not get back at all if that Spaniard proved a genuine killer.

All she muttered was, 'I'm not happy, Carl.'

With the actual fight now just hours away it started dawning on me what I'd committed to and I began to feel a bit nervous for the first time. I'd done some hard training but three weeks isn't long to prepare for a no-rules fight that might be to the death.

Dan picked me up in his Transit van. It was a Friday night. No fancy Jags and promoters in sheepskin coats this time. The two minders – both armed in case of emergencies – followed behind in a car.

Less than half an hour later, we pulled into an industrial park near Dagenham Old Docks, next to a KFC, and Dan simply said, 'We're here'. I noticed dim lights through a big open door into a warehouse and then saw the headlight beams of loads of cars gathered around inside.

As we drove in, I also saw there wasn't a cage in sight. It was an open arena. I'd thought it was going to be a closed arena, at least a cattle shed to keep the fighters hemmed in. Dan didn't say a word but I could tell he was as surprised as me. But it was too late to turn round and leave.

Lots of heavy looking characters were standing around by their cars which all had their headlights on full beam. It looked just like the opening to that Michael Caine film *Shiner*, which I'd worked on as a consultant.

I was already well hyped up and couldn't wait to get started so I got straight out of the van just as a big black Merc with smoked-out windows glided into the warehouse. The fat Spaniard got out of it. Flash bastard was behaving as if he'd already won. I ignored him and got into the arena and began warming up. I was wearing thin layer bag gloves with cut away fingers so I could still grab him when I wanted. There were no rules about gloves although obviously I couldn't have got away with wearing knuckle dusters!

Meanwhile the fat Spaniard was lumbering around as if he owned the place, with three or four blokes around him for protection. As I looked across at him, I'll swear he had a bit of onion ring hanging out of the corner of his mouth so I shouted at him, 'You still eatin'?'

It was just a bit of harmless theatre although from the look on his face he didn't get the joke at all – but I'll swear he checked just to see if there was any food on his face.

Then the Spaniard moved towards me, frowning to try and look like a tough nut. It was pathetic. He was in jeans, boots and badly fitted t-shirt and his belly was bursting out all over the place. I had this tight khaki t-shirt with full army trousers from a surplus store and it made me look like a squaddie. I even had on black army boots.

So he walked across from one corner of the arena to the other and then suddenly starts charging towards me like a flabby rhino. I side-stepped him and banged him straight in the ear as he passed and he went sideways onto the floor. Then he got up and charged again. This time I moved the other way and banged him on the other ear. It was all so bloody easy.

The fat bastard was stumbling all over the floor after that second hit. He couldn't cope with it. Then I got him square on the nose, which then burst like a balloon. Bits of gristle flying in all directions. Blood streaming down his face. I even stepped back for a moment to let him compose himself. I must have been going soft with old age.

Then he charged right at me but I side-stepped him and as he passed each time I kneed him straight in the ribs. The third time he went crashing to the floor and I steamed in and crunched on his neck. Then I smacked him a couple of times and he went out like a light. No one stopped the fight. I just stopped myself. I could have carried on mashing his head but that's not my scene. I'd finished the job already so there was no need to kill the geezer. He was out cold. End of story.

Now we had to get out of that arena in double quick time. I couldn't believe how easy it had been. In less than three and a half minutes I'd copped ten grand. Trouble was that once the fat Spaniard had hit the floor bottles started flying in because these punters were angry at having lost a few bob. If I'd been in a cage like normal I'd have been perfectly safe because whatever they threw at you, it wouldn't actually hit you. But this was seriously hazardous. I was also so hyped up I'd started taunting the customers which didn't help. The crowd were going berserk because they'd put all their money on the fat Spaniard. They'd never even heard of me. There were screams of 'fix' because these sorts of characters don't like losing their hard earned cash. In some ways it was a rougher, younger crowd than usual.

In the middle of all this bedlam, I was relieved to notice Dan walking straight over to the promoter and getting my money on the spot. He then beckoned me over and I wiped my sweat-drenched nose and we marched off towards the van. Trouble was that the crowd was now going completely AWOL.

As a mob of blokes encircled us I just managed to pile into the Transit front seat. Our two minders scrambled into the car behind us and we drove out of that warehouse at high speed.

Dan was as calm as ever and all he said to me was, 'Where d'you want to go, son?'

'Home,' I said.

And that was it. Easiest £10,000 I ever earned in me life.

Less than an hour later I was walking up the garden path to my house with hardly a scratch on me. Carole ripped open the door before my boot touched the doorstep.

I walked calmly past her and slapped all the cash down on the kitchen table and said, 'There's yer money.'

'It couldn't have been that easy?' she asked suspiciously.

'Easy as pie.'

Carole didn't exactly give me a hug and a kiss on the spot, but seeing I was in one piece made it easier for her to forget how I'd defied her and gone back into the fight game. I was feeling on top of the moon. I'd just earned more in less than three minutes than I could earn in three months in the building trade. The old fight bug had bitten and now my biggest problem was resisting the temptation to have another lucrative scrap.

# Epilogue: Last Man Standing

Everything back at home seemed to return to normal really quickly. I guess Carole was relieved to see I hadn't been hurt and she'd forgiven me although I stayed in training. When she had a dig at me about it I just said, 'I dunno why I'm still training. I just want to stay fit, babes.' But in the back of my mind I was still thinking about the fight game. Maybe she knew that all along?

Surprise, surprise. Just two weeks after mashing that fat Spaniard to pieces I got offered more work. It just ain't that easy to turn your back on it.

Truth is I really fancied my chances and my promoter mate Dan had already made it clear there might be more work on the way home after I'd beaten that fat Spaniard.

Then two weeks later I got a call from Dan.

'I got one lined up, son,' he said. 'Younger fella and it's gonna be in Southend.'

I didn't ask much else except, 'Do we have to have a meet with him?'

'No. I ain't seen him but I heard he's quite a fit geezer. A kick boxer about 28 or 30, something like that.'

I didn't really take on board what he was saying there and then because I was still on a high at the time. I wasn't worried. I reckoned I could take anyone on without a problem.

But I didn't dare tell Carole because I knew this time she'd really kill me if she found out.

The fight was scheduled for two weeks later. I was already fit from training for the last dust-up so I didn't really care when it was going to be. Dan said the money was the same and so were the promoters. But none of that interested me. I should have known better.

Back at home Carole had put the money from the last fight in the bank. Meanwhile I was still eating special food and I'd completely knocked the beer on the head, which was what really bothered her. She sensed something was happening but she couldn't be sure what it was. But I chose to stay quiet again.

\* \* \*

The fight was on a Saturday night and that morning I had a run and went down the gym before eating a massive pasta lunch. Then at about six o'clock I just blurted it out to Carole. 'I'm just poppin' out for a while.'

And she went, 'What, on a Saturday?'

I took a big gulp and thought, 'Oh well, in for a penny…'

'To tell you the truth I got another fight on tonight.'

I could see the steam building up inside her head as my words sunk in.

And it didn't help much when I added, 'Don't worry, babes, I'll be back in two hours.'

That's when she screamed and gave me a slap. Thank God the kids were upstairs in their bedroom at the time so they didn't hear a thing.

Carole said she'd had enough and called me a lying bastard and everything else under the sun, which I thoroughly deserved. She was angrier than I had ever seen her but she didn't try and stop me. She just said, 'Get out! Get out and don't ever come back.'

I was being such a selfish bastard I deserved to be divorced there and then. All I could think about was myself, not Carole and the kids. But that's what being hyped up for a fight does to you. I kept telling myself I was doing it for the money, which would go towards the future of my kids. I wanted the money for them. I honestly did.

So I walked out of the house with Carole still screaming and blocked it all out of my mind. I was focused on only one thing – that fight. I got in my Volvo shaking with rage and drove off not knowing if I'd have a family to come back to later that evening.

It took me under forty minutes to get to Southend, where I was due to meet Dan near the town's famous pier. I soon spotted him waiting in his van and joined him. This time those same two minders were in the back of Dan's vehicle, packing tools once again.

We drove off to another industrial park and a few minutes later turned up a sloping entrance towards a warehouse. Through the small entrance I could see it was all lit up inside. As we drove in, we passed forklift trucks and boxes scattered across the concrete floor.

This time there was a cage of sorts consisting of metal fencing with concrete blocks holding it down like you get on building sites. It had been arranged like an eight-sided cage without a roof.

Anyway, we pulled up next to it and suddenly all these car headlights outside the cage lit up. It was very theatrical and dramatic. I'd been in a lot weirder places than this so I wasn't bothered by any of it. But this time there were a lot more people than usual.

I got out of Dan's van and walked straight towards the cage where some big fat bald-headed geezer dragged the fence with the concrete weights open for me to go in. I was in the same khaki gear I wore against the fat Spaniard which I now considered to be lucky after my last fight.

My opponent was already in there kicking around and when I first caught sight of him I thought, 'Fuckin' hell. He looks fit.' He was about my height, my sort of weight but clearly fitter and younger than me. Maybe this wasn't going to be as easy as I'd presumed.

He looked a bit eastern European although I never actually found out his name let alone where he came from. Anyway, I continued into the cage as the fat bloke dragged the gate shut.

Now we're off.

My opponent came straight at me, kicking out skilfully and quickly. I was on the floor in seconds. Then I punched upwards from the floor into his bollocks to try and slow him down only to find he had a bloody box on. So I grabbed at his box and started to drag him over. Then he kicked me very accurately on the chin as he finally tumbled over. I felt two of my teeth clatter together and snap as his kick connected with my face. Later I realised they'd flown out of my mouth, although I didn't notice any of this at the time.

After my opponent finally fell to the ground I rolled onto him and pushed my hand into his head and tried to knock him out. I knew he was a lot stronger and fitter than me and I had to get it over quickly or else I was dead meat. So I smacked him hard in the ribs with my cut-off fingerless gloves just like the ones I wore in the fight against the fat Spaniard.

But it didn't stop him much and within moments we'd both managed to get to our feet and were having a proper full-on fist fight. I preferred standing up to laying down any day of the week. Now we were both heavily committed to a form of stand-off. First he kicked me really hard as I tried to strike out with my fists. I kept trying to reach him only for him to catch me with yet another painful kick to the ribs. This kid really knew his stuff. I knew I needed to bide my time and try to pick the perfect moment to strike out but for the moment he was completely running the show.

Then my opponent momentarily lifted his head just a touch too high and, bang, I got him straight in the throat with the back of my hand and down he went. I steamed into him on the floor like rolling thunder and trod all over him. Then I leaned down and started smacking him just to make sure he had no chance of reviving. After a right pummelling he was finally out cold.

It was that jab to the throat which won it for me. As we'd been scrapping during that stand-up, he'd just lifted his head high enough and I'd got him. Up until then he'd hardly put a foot wrong. I'd seen my opportunity and taken it.

Now I looked down at him crumpled on the floor and

hesitated for a split second. His breathing looked a bit strange but I couldn't risk him coming back at me a second time because I was close to exhaustion myself.

So I just tore into him and hurt him very badly on the knees, legs, head, you name it. This was about me or him. I just kept hitting him over and over again to make sure he couldn't come back again. I was oblivious to the jeering crowd spitting blood because they'd once again lost a small fortune on their man.

The car lights were still illuminating the scene with him lying flat on his face out cold. I pulled him round to take a look at him and put my hand on his mouth to make sure he was breathing. Thank God he was.

The whole fight had lasted about ten minutes but it had felt like two hours. I'd got a severe beating, no denying it. I was lucky to still be standing.

The crowd was getting noisier and I looked around for Dan. Luckily he was already at the gate and pulled it open and we all jumped in the van pronto. It was chaos. They were throwing bottles and stuff at the van. As we screeched out of the warehouse exit, I turned to look back at the makeshift cage and saw three geezers leaning over my opponent trying to revive him. I never even knew his name.

It was only then I realised the full extent of my injuries. I couldn't even see properly out of either eye so I asked Steve to drive me straight home. I was fully conscious but I couldn't talk properly either. I didn't care about my car, which was still parked on a meter near Southend Pier.

Dan asked me if I wanted him to take me to a doctor but I

just mumbled through my bleeding mouth. 'Nah. Just wanna go home.'

Inside the van, Dan towelled me down and I tried to drink a bit of water but my outfit was soaked in claret. I looked in a dreadful state.

Steve eventually dropped me outside my house and I stumbled up the pathway before staggering in through the front door. Steve didn't hang around to see me in. He didn't know Carole and he never would.

It was about eleven and thank God Carole was in bed when I crept in. Then I fell up the stairs and took off all my clothes and jumped in the shower. That's when I saw myself in the mirror for the first time and looked back at the Elephant Man. I thought fuckin' hell, Carole will kill me! I knew I'd taken a few whacks but I didn't realise how bad it was until then.

I knew I couldn't hide my injuries from Carole but I didn't want to wake her up so I crept back down the stairs to my little office at the back of the house and collapsed in my armchair. I took loads of paracetamol to try and kill the pain and just sat there and suffered. I deserved it for being such a selfish arsehole.

I kept thinking of what I'd done and how I'd let Carole and the girls down so badly. I was in a right state. I had done a wrong deed and now I was preparing for her to divorce me. I was also afraid the girls – Jaime was six and Mel ten by this time – would be so scared when they saw me.

A few hours later as the sun was coming up, Carole looked in the office and burst into tears the moment she saw me.

'What have you done to yerself?'

I could barely talk, my mouth was so sore. When I tried to say sorry a load of blood bubbled out of my mouth. It was pathetic.

Then Carole started screaming. It was ear-piercing stuff born more out of frustration than anger. I was driving her mad and this was obviously the last straw.

The girls had remained in their bedroom until now but they came down when Carole began screaming. I told her to keep them away from me because I was so worried about what they might think. They didn't deserve this. Nor did Carole.

Then Jaime caught a glimpse of me through the crack in the office door and started screaming. I mumbled something about how I'd run into someone's hand but I'm not sure she could hear me above all the noise in any case.

Somehow, through all the hysteria and crying I managed to earn some sympathy from Carole and instead of screaming divorce at me she started looking after me and helping me to recover. She put me straight to bed and asked if I wanted a doctor. At first I refused but the pain got so bad the next day that I went to my GP because I couldn't breathe. When he asked me what happened I said I got run over. He just looked at my hands and fists and shook his head in disbelief.

I then had to go and have my ribs and hands x-rayed at Basildon Hospital. I had a face x-ray as well but luckily I only had hairline cracks and lot of bruises but no actual breaks. The doc in the hospital even pointed out I had some gristle in there because those ribs had been broken a few times before. They all knew only too well that I'd been in a serious scrap.

Even now when I lift my arm too high it still hurts. Amazingly, my face was alright apart from the missing teeth. I never found them. And that piece of plastic put in my face all those years earlier had somehow survived so I was quite lucky in a way, although my hands were like balloons for about two weeks.

Dan the man turned up with my money the very next day. He refused to come into the house and chucked it through the letterbox instead. He didn't even take his usual percentage out of it although I'm sure he was getting something from the other side as well.

A few days later I rang Dan and told him for the very last time: 'Never again.'

I know he'll try and pull me back in for another fight, but this time it really is the end of my career.

Carole said my excuse that the money was for the kids was pathetic but at least we've put it away for them. Deep down I felt I'd learned a lesson and that now I had nothing to prove to anyone. Now I've done it I can sleep easy in my bed at nights. I had forgotten what pain was like and never want to feel this way again as long as I live.

If I'd had it too easy in that second fight I might have been sucked into carrying on. Meeting such a tough opponent was a good thing. I thought about my opponent after the fight but I had to remain detached from anything to do with him otherwise it would have done my head in. I know for a fact he didn't die because I specially asked Dan to find out and he said he was just badly bruised. 'He'll kick on again. Don't worry about him,' added Dan. I hoped he was telling me the truth.

That fight has taken a lot out of me because you don't heal so quickly when you're older. I'd also got a timely reminder that I wasn't so invincible after all.

I even promised Carole I'd change my phone number so I wasn't tempted ever again. The girls still haven't got a clue what

I was up to. They just think that daddy got into a fight in a pub. Teachers at their school have read about me and know what I used to do. No doubt my daughter Mel will get her hands on this book one day and find out all about her old man. I hope she doesn't think less of me when she learns the truth.

Things are back to normal again at home. I'm working in the building trade once again and I'm in one piece, thank God. That's it. This time I ain't going back in The Cage. I'm definitely too old for this game.

End of story.